A Consumer Society

ISSUES

Volume 43

Editor

Craig Donnellan

Independence

Educational Publishers
Cambridge

First published by Independence
PO Box 295
Cambridge CB1 3XP
England

British Library Cataloguing in Publication Data
A Consumer Society – (Issues Series)
I. Donnellan, Craig II. Series
381.3

ISBN 1 86168 204 2

Printed in Great Britain
The Burlington Press
Cambridge

Typeset by
Claire Boyd

Cover
The illustration on the front cover is by
Pumpkin House.

CONTENTS

Chapter One: Consumer Trends

Chapter Two: Consumer Awareness

Introduction

A *Consumer Society* is the forty-third volume in the Issues series. The aim of this series is to offer up-to-date information about important issues in our world.

A *Consumer Society* examines consumer trends and consumer rights.

The information comes from a wide variety of sources and includes:
Government reports and statistics
Newspaper reports and features
Magazine articles and surveys
Literature from lobby groups
and charitable organisations.

It is hoped that, as you read about the many aspects of the issues explored in this book, you will critically evaluate the information presented. It is important that you decide whether you are being presented with facts or opinions. Does the writer give a biased or an unbiased report? If an opinion is being expressed, do you agree with the writer?

A *Consumer Society* offers a useful starting-point for those who need convenient access to information about the many issues involved. However, it is only a starting-point. At the back of the book is a list of organisations which you may want to contact for further information.

*****

Consumers splash out in 'feelgood revolution'

By John Arlidge

Feeling good? You should. For the first time, Britons are spending more on having fun than on staying alive.

Consumers are splashing out one-third more on going out, holidays and entertainment than on eating, drinking and health. The 'feelgood revolution' is the biggest shift in spending since records began 50 years ago.

Spending on 'luxuries' – restaurants, entertainment, leisure, and holidays – reached £110 billion last year, dwarfing the £80bn spent on 'essentials' – food and drink, household goods, toiletries and medical services.

The new figures, from consumer analysts Mintel, reveal that the Christmas and New Year spending boom, which surprised retailers and economists, was no blip – it was the latest chapter in the longest spending spree Britain has ever seen.

'Wants have replaced needs,' says James McCoy, the analyst who carried out the research. 'Consumers have more than enough money for the basics of life and are now spending with abandon on life's luxuries.'

In 1991, Britons spent £60bn on food and drink, household goods and health, compared with £56bn on 'fun'. By last year, that situation had reversed.

Britons spent a massive £40bn on holidays in 2001 – up from £20bn in 1991. Some £24bn was spent in restaurants. Spending in cinemas doubled while theatre suffered a small decline. Thanks to the National Lottery, the amount spent on gambling more than doubled to £7.5bn.

Music sales increased twofold. Sales of sporting goods trebled to £10bn. Health and fitness, including gym membership, increased by 110 per cent to £1.2bn.

Allowing for inflation, overall spending on luxuries has risen by a massive 50 per cent over the past decade. Spending on 'essentials' was up by just 7 per cent. Spending on some basics – notably food, general household goods and clothes – has fallen in real terms.

The 'feelgood' spending spree has been fuelled by rising wages, falling prices, and low interest rates. 'Consumers are wealthier than ever, their homes are worth more, and low interest rates make it cheaper than ever to borrow money,' McCoy says.

While earnings have risen, competition between manufacturers and retailers has forced down prices of many essentials. Food prices have remained static over the past decade while the price of basic clothes has dropped.

'When you look at the whole range of products we buy in the high street we are paying a lot less for them than we were even five years ago,' McCoy says. 'That gives wealthy consumers more cash to spend on even more essentials or on luxuries. Most of us are choosing to spend more on the good things in life.'

While the cost of essentials has fallen, the price of luxury goods has remained high as brand owners have used marketing and celebrity endorsement to convince consumers that logos and high prices mean exclusivity and quality.

Decreasing leisure time has also encouraged spending. 'People may be better off but they have less time to themselves,' McCoy says. 'Consumers are determined to make the best of the free time they do have. If you only have an hour or two to yourself in the morning or after work, you make sure you enjoy it – even if that means spending hundreds of pounds a year on a gym or on going out to eat.'

Despite warnings from politicians and economists that consumer spending and debt are too high and Britain is heading for a crash, consumers show no signs of slowing down.

One of the fastest growing sectors in the past decade has been financial services, the study shows. The more consumers spend, the more they want to make sure their money works even harder – so they can spend even more in the future.

• The above article appeared in *The Observer*, 27 January 2002.

No time like the present for debts, drink and decorating

By Felicity Lawrence,
Consumer Affairs
Correspondent

People are spending more on wine, spirits and convenience foods than ever, and to counteract the ravages of their intensive lifestyle then buy a record number of beauty products, vitamin pills and over-the-counter medicines.

Personal disposable income has risen by 30% in real terms over the past 10 years, but the average debt for every man, woman and child is now £11,830. Personal debt rose to £720bn in 2001, encouraged by low and stable interest rates.

Nearly a third of people are concerned about their financial situation, according to a survey of lifestyles and consumer spending published by Mintel yesterday. But two-thirds were either happy about it or had not thought about how their circumstances might be affected by the global economy.

There has been a 24-percentage-point drop since 1992 in the number of adults who would save money in a bank or building society when they felt financially confident. Instead, the trend over the past 10 years has been to spend more on ourselves, although that trend has slowed slightly since 1997.

But there are also signs of prudence: spending on financial services is growing fastest, as people invest in life insurance and personal pensions.

The number of older men is growing relative to the number of older women, as the life expectancy gap between the sexes narrows. The next decade will see fewer single old women and more old couples, who are likely to spend more on leisure and travel together.

The next five years will also see a growth of 3% in the number of 15 to 34-year-olds without dependants, who as first-time buyers of houses and services will stimulate growth.

Forecast spending among these two groups makes Mintel bullish about the economy generally.

Mintel interviewed 2,000 adults immediately after the events of September 11 and again last November.

- Average debt per man, woman and child £11,830
- Spending on wine to drink at home up 47% in five years
- Consumption of spirits up 20% in five years
- Convenience food market up 41% since 1992
- Spending on home furnishings up 19% to £10.3bn
- More couples survive together into old age
- Average size of households down to 2.23

The size of the average household is still falling, as divorce rates rise; down to 2.23 people from 2.65 people 10 years ago. More than half of households now have a computer, compared with under one in three in 1995. The value of the mobile phone market has increased by 439% in the past five years, and is now close to saturation point.

Spending on home furnishings has risen by 19% over the past 10 years to £10.3bn in 2001, stimulated by the popularity of TV decorating programmes. And as people stay home to enjoy the results, drinking and entertaining at home are on the increase.

Consumption of wine at home was up 47% last year against five years ago. Consumption of spirits, which declined by 9% between 1991 and 1996, has grown by over 20% in the past five years as flavoured mixed drinks have become fashionable among younger groups.

People are also spending more to buy time: expenditure on domestic and garden help has grown 88% in five years at current prices to £4.9bn, while the convenience meal market has grown 41% in real terms over 10 years. A fifth of adults rarely sit down for a meal.

Men's spending on toiletries was 21% up in real terms in 2001, compared with five years ago. Women too continue to spend more on beauty products, but only 4% more.

Insights into consumer markets

Here are just a few facts and insights into consumer markets and society which we hope will interest and, in some cases, even surprise you. It draws on work within MORI futures – a joint service from MORI and Market Dynamics

Last year, Tesco took more money in an average week (£355m)[1] than was spent throughout the entire year in the UK on all goods and services bought over the internet.

Cut through the hype and overvalued share prices and the reality is that only 23% of British households currently have access to the internet.[2] The UK lags far behind the US and much of continental Europe in terms of household internet access. While the internet will have a profound influence in the next millennium, do not expect it to revolutionise business overnight; as yet, nobody has really found a reliable way of generating profits from people online.

Cruises have doubled their share of the UK outbound holiday market in the space of 5 years. Last year an estimated 630,000 Britons took a cruise holiday.[3]

This is just one example of how demographic change is positively impacting patterns of consumption. In particular, growth in the number of affluent 45-54-year-olds is changing spending patterns right across the retail and leisure sectors.

However, a negative impact of demographic change is the increase in economic dependency ratios; currently each pensioner in the UK is supported by three people in work but by 2030 those same three working people will be supporting two pensioners.

Stella Artois is now the UK's most valuable beer brand and second only to Carling in terms of volume sales.[4]

How can a 'premium' product – in

all senses of the word – now be the beer of mainstream choice? Good advertising and luck no doubt play a part. So too do growing consumer spending power, an ageing pub-going population and increasing holiday exposure to stronger continental lagers.

The deeper message is that consumer society changes at an increasingly rapid pace. Premium and mainstream markets become harder to define. Yesterday's innovative, high-quality convenience food from M&S becomes today's ubiquitous supermarket ready-meal.

By the year 2000, there will be more men aged 35-44 than aged 25-34 in the UK population.[5]

What is more, in a reversal of the pattern of the 1990s, there will be more men in their early and mid thirties than women in their late twenties – the age cohorts from which men and women traditionally draw their partners. This could lead to a new generation of Brian rather than Bridget Jones.

Amid increasing signs of recovery in the High Street, retail sales of household goods are now increasing by more than 7% per year but food sales are virtually static.[6]

Not only does this divergence of performance reflect the strength of the housing market and demand for new computer and phone products, it also illustrates a more fundamental shift of consumer spending power away from 'essentials' towards 'luxuries'.

6.6 million people in the United Kingdom – 24% of all those in employment – usually work more than 45 hours per week while 2.3 million (9%) usually work more than 55 hours per week.[7]

While IT is meant to have heralded a new age of leisure, the reality for many of those in full-time jobs is that they are working harder and harder. As well as increasing levels of stress and time pressure this will continue to fuel demand for products and services designed to save time, take away everyday hassles and serve people on the move.

East Anglia is the UK's most heavily 'superstored' region with a population of only 50,000 people for each grocery superstore compared with a national average of 55,000 people per store.[8]

The reality is that with out-of-town planning permission harder to come by and most regions approaching saturation coverage, the future development of grocery retailing lies in the rebirth of High Street stores and innovative convenience formats.

In 1998, 3.4 million Britons took long haul (non-European) holidays in the Rest of the World outside North America compared with only 2.6 million taking holidays in North America itself.[9]

Apart from simple economics, several wide-ranging consumer trends are driving increasingly adventurous holiday taking behaviour to destinations outside Europe and the English-speaking world: greater confidence; an increasing desire among society's 30% of leading edge consumers to differentiate themselves from their peers and an increasing willingness to spend on worthwhile experiences rather than physical possessions

Almost three in ten British people claim to have either chosen or boycotted a product or service on ethical grounds in the past 12 months.[10]

The current debate about genetically modified food testing in Britain clearly demonstrates the strength of consumer pressure. A majority believe that GM foods are not beneficial to society and are unclear about scientists' objectives in developing this type of food.[11]

The population of the South-East of the UK is expected to increase by a further 13% over the next 20 years.[12]

Faced with the reality of better job prospects and higher wages, the population of the North and North-West of the UK looks set to continue its now established pattern of southwards migration. Without regeneration of the urban centres of the North, the South-East can expect more house price inflation, greater congestion and increasing pressure on public services – schools, hospitals, transport etc.

It is estimated that in today's Britain, 50% of the country's marketable wealth in the household sector belongs to just 10% of the population.[13] In the same society, between 1.5 and 2

million people aged over 21 were earning sufficiently little to be affected by the introduction of a statutory minimum wage of £3.60 per hour.[14]

Inequality of income and wealth is not a new phenomenon in British society. The co-existence of 20% plus house price inflation in some parts of London and houses which literally cannot be sold at any price in parts of Greater Manchester, reflects a divergence of individual experience and opportunity which will persist well into the next century.

Organised crime is now Britain's third largest industry worth £50 billion a year.[15]

As well as having an impact on economic activity in Britain, crime is permeating our value system. Four in ten people claim that they would knowingly purchase a counterfeit product if the price and quality of the goods is acceptable[16] and 28% of Britons aged 15-24 think that everyone should try banned drugs at least once in their lives.[17]

Sources:

1. Tesco Annual Report, 1998
2. MORI Omnibus aggregate data, 1999
3. Passenger Shipping Association 1998
4. Euromonitor 1999, Whitbread PLC
5. Government Actuary's Department, Population Trends No. 91, Spring 1998
6. ONS Retail Sales First Release to June 1999
7. Labour Force Quarterly Supplement, Summer 1999
8. IGD, 1999, MORI futures' analysis of company reports
9. International Passenger Survey 1999
10. MORI Corporate Social Responsibility survey among 1,983 GB adults aged 15+, July-August 1998
11. Survey among 1,109 adults aged 16+ interviewed in March-April 1999 on the People's Panel, for the Office of Science and Technology of the Department of Trade and Industry
12. ONS Regional Population Trends, August 1999
13. Inland Revenue, Social Trends 1999
14. Labour Force Survey/New Earnings Survey, Social Trends 1999
15. National Criminal Intelligence Service report, 1999
16. Survey for the Anti-Counterfeiting Group, on the MORI Omnibus among 996 adults aged 15+ in September 1997
17. MORI Socioconsult Monitor among 1,700 GB adults aged 15+, April-June 1997

- The above information is from MORI's web site at www.mori.com

© MORI

Average weekly expenditure on the main commodities and services

Leisure goods and services were the largest item of spending by an increased margin, with an average of £70 a week

Commodity / service	Average weekly expenditure
Leisure goods & services	£70.40
Housing	£63.90
Food & non-alcoholic drinks	£61.90
Motoring	£55.10
Household goods & services	£54.60
Clothing & footwear	£22.00
Alcoholic drink	£15.00
Personal goods & services	£14.70
Fuel & power	£11.90
Fares & other travel costs	£9.50
Tobacco	£6.10
Miscellaneous	£0.70

All amounts are rounded to the nearest 10p

Source: 'Family Spending in the United Kingdom 2000-01', ONS, Crown Copyright

Shopping daze

Shopping daze zombies who don't know what they're buying. Why we lose control at the supermarket

Walking through the doors of a supermarket turns shoppers into zombies.

Eighty per cent of the decisions made as they trawl through the aisles are subconscious, a study has found.

Researchers who videoed 125,000 shoppers over 10 years found they often went home with six times more items that they intended to buy.

Many of the purchases they couldn't even remember choosing.

Items were picked up because of subconscious 'prompts' such as lighting, colour and the strategic positioning of well-known brands, the researchers found.

In regularly visited stores, shoppers always followed the same route, covering only a third of the store, even though they believed they had walked around the entire shop.

Even entering the store was a preordained matter. Most shoppers automatically turned left as they walked in.

Psychologists believe this can be traced back to Stone Age times, when it was important to have the stronger right arm facing any potential attacker.

Stores are keen to cash in on this tendency, according to researchers, by placing their best deals to the left of the entrance.

Siemon Scamell-Katz of ID Magasin, which carried out the study, said: 'People do most of their shopping in a daze.

'Shopping is often a chore and people would rather be doing something else, so they switch off and follow learnt patterns of behaviour.

'In supermarkets, that often means they end up buying a lot of goods they did not intend to buy.'

ID Magasin's video footage also showed that the colour and texture of a shop's flooring can stop customers from entering the store.

If the flooring contrasts too much with external flooring in a shopping centre, the difference acts as a mental 'barrier' that prevents customers from breaking through.

'If there is a line, people tend not to cross it,' said Mr Scamell-Katz. He said a new Burtons and Dorothy Perkins store in a shopping centre in Uxbridge, West London, had deliberately continued the mall's flooring inside the shop to encourage shoppers inside.

'Shopping is often a chore and people would rather be doing something else, so they switch off and follow learnt patterns of behaviour'

Back in the supermarket, shoppers usually arrived with about ten items on their shopping list. On average, they left with 60.

They were prompted to buy certain types of foods when they spotted brands and logos they recognised.

If they saw the familiar red and white of a Coca-Cola bottle for example, many started loading their trolley with soft drinks, without even realising.

Mr Scamell-Katz said: 'Retailers want to try and keep people in this "zombie" mode while they're shopping.

'To do this they make sure items are always in the same part of the store and encourage shoppers to buy certain categories of goods by displaying well-known brands in a prominent position.'

In clothes stores, shoppers make a lot of their decisions by touch.

'A woman browsing in a fashion store will typically touch about 15 items,' said Mr Scamell-Katz.

'Psychologists have proved that touching a garment helps us to visualise what it will look like when it is on.

'We get an idea of the weight of the fabric and how it might hang.'

© *The Daily Mail, 2001*

Commercial pressure

The children's view

Written and conceived by
Jenina Bas

Without thinking about it – and without children realising it – most parents offer their children a sound education in becoming consumers from a very young age. One parent said that exposing children to advertising, and discussing it with them, gave young people 'an inoculation' against it. Indeed, many of the day-to-day activities that parents do with their children, from watching TV to going shopping, are important ways in which young people are introduced to the commercial aspects of the modern world and learn to operate in it. This is reflected by the memories of older children who recall shopping tantrums and other similar behaviour, which often resulted in being 'told off' or taken out of the shop unceremoniously. Equally, they refer to parental examples as the way that they learned about the ins and outs of shopping, cooking and watching TV.

- Older children also recall a wide range of routine experiences which act as early practical lessons. This can include anything – from playing with a toy cooking set or a cash till, carefully choosing what to buy with pocket money, or making a cake instead of buying one, to saving up and choosing a present for a member of the family or a friend, or even just going along with their parents on a shopping trip. Virtually all children old enough to talk can remember a time when their parents refused to buy them something because it was too expensive, too 'grown-up' or 'not good for you'.
- Tantrums and nagging at such refusals gradually disappear as children get older and develop both an understanding that they cannot have everything they want as well as an ability to reach a compromise. 'I can offer to pay for some of it with my pocket money' or 'I can offer to do something around the house that I don't normally do', are negotiating tactics that two children said worked from time to time!
- The experience of trying out a promoted new product only to be disappointed is also a widely shared experience amongst older children. This results in a healthy scepticism about all advertising. 'Ads always make things look really yummy, but sometimes you try it and it's awful or not as nice as the one you're already buying,' was the view of one 12-year-old, whose friends all nodded in agreement.
- Children recall their own experiences when considering how parents can best deal with commercial pressure. Common responses and recommendations were: 'Don't take children shopping all the time', 'Don't spoil them' and 'Be firm'.
- However, it would be wrong to conclude from older children's understanding of the commercial process that today's generation are unrealistically virtuous. When negotiating with their parents, older children are well aware of the value of having a product that they want endorsed by their friend and, better still, other adults – not least the other parent! As one 13-year-old put it, 'If Mum won't get it, I'll talk Dad into it.'
- The tendency to rebel and be different becomes more evident in the middle-teens when, for example, fast foods become the usual food consumed with friends, and movies and videos with an adult age rating become appealing. Also, from around the age of 11, specific ideas about which brands of, for example, shoes and clothes are fashionable become

more important, often as part of the change from childhood to adulthood. Not surprisingly, therefore, some parents feel that 'I have no influence on the teenagers . . .'

- There's been a good deal of research into the way children make decisions about things they want to buy and judgments about things that are marketed and advertised. A psychological study at Exeter University into food preferences points to children naturally categorising different foods according to whether they are seen to be 'healthy' or 'unhealthy', whether they are best eaten as meals or as snacks, and whether they are raw or cooked and processed in some way. It concluded that by around the age of seven to eight, children have a good basic understanding of different foods and what makes up a healthy diet.

- This is also around the age that they begin to know what being a 'good' consumer in the family context is all about and when they consciously start to realise that, 'I used to make a fuss in shops when I wanted something, but I don't do it now'. 'Take no nonsense, and occasionally let them [the children] win,' was the advice of a 17-year-old to any parent, which is surprisingly in tune with the view of a mother who said, 'Don't make a drama out of it. Ads are part of life and the more you attract attention to them, the more attractive they become.'

- The preferences of children and young people for certain types of food and other products change as they grow older, reflecting the different stages of children's social development. In the same way that dolls and toy diggers might give way to clothes and computer games as children grow older, sweets might give way to fast foods as the kind of things that are enjoyed amongst friends.

Parents tend to fall into two camps in this respect

Some worry at all stages about their children eating too many sweets or

Key points
- Many family activities, from watching TV to going shopping, enable children to learn about the commercial aspects of the modern world
- As they grow up, children realise they cannot have everything, they learn to negotiate and compromise, and their tastes and preferences change and develop
- The home and family environment is an important source of values, as well as information and knowledge on topics not fully covered at school

having too many toy guns. Others recognise that they need to meet their children part of the way and agree to things like a television in their child's bedroom. Generally, however, there is a recognition that a great deal of a child's day-to-day activities, including eating, are still very much within the family environment and therefore within the influence of parents.

- **Victor, 8, . . .**
has a younger brother of three. He says: 'I don't really ask for anything much except football stuff. Anyway, my mum doesn't have much time for shopping and tells me things are expensive.' But later on, he remembers there are occasions that he gets the kind of things he does like – 'Oh yeah, at Christmas and stuff'. He says he no longer has tantrums, in shops or anywhere else, but eagerly offers his younger brother as an example of somebody who does. 'He cries and moans and my mum just has to stop him.' Victor says his mother generally does the shopping and cooking. 'We just eat what she buys . . . we eat lots of rice and she tells us to eat our vegetables up and that sweets aren't good for our teeth

---

Most parents offer their children a sound education in becoming consumers from a very young age

---

. . . I can usually wait for tea to be cooked, but when my brother gets hungry and starts to moan she'll give him a piece of bread or fruit or carrot or something.'

- **Grace, 13, . . .**
says that she still has 'tantrums' of a sort – 'I don't scream and cry and stuff, but I know I stomp and sulk when I don't get what I want.' She recalls a recent incident when both her mother and father would not buy her a pair of shoes with four-inch heels. But she also says there are times 'when I can see their point. Like that time last year when I wanted a pet. My mum said no because she didn't think I could look after it myself, and when I thought about it, she was probably right. Anyway, if I really want to buy something they won't buy for me, I can save up for it.' Her mother does most of the cooking, but she and her father also sometimes get involved at weekends or on special occasions. She lets her mum know what she would like to eat so that she can buy it, but 'I sometimes go shopping with her and just put things in the trolley . . . she doesn't really mind as long as we eat it.'

- **Ben, 17, . . .**
can't recall a recent incident when he disagreed with his parents about what to buy. 'Situations like that happened when I was younger, but they don't happen now because they get me the things I need – like for school and stuff – plus other reasonable things, and if there's anything I really want that they won't get me, I can get it for myself because I work part-time.' He still eats most of his meals at home and occasionally helps in the cooking. 'My mum knows more or less what I like and I sometimes tell her what I feel like eating, if she asks, but I don't do the shopping with her or anything. Sometimes I help her carry the shopping in or something.'

From home to school
With children spending well under half of their waking time at school, the importance of learning in the family environment is becoming more and more recognised. As the

head of a secondary school explained, 'There is little enough time in the school day to cover the core subjects of the National Curriculum, but even if there was, teachers can only effectively teach the basic aspects that fall under personal and social development – like nutrition and cooking, or learning about the way advertising exists to persuade and present only one side of the story. But whatever we do needs to work with the values and habits that come from the home.'

Indeed, older children's responses consistently place family (especially mothers), friends and teachers as influential sources of information on commercial life. Some parents are even aware of the way that older children are able to help introduce their younger brothers or sisters to, for example, different types of foods. 'She [a six-year-old] learns a lot from her older sister. She tells her to eat her vegetables, not to eat too many chocolates and things like that,' said one mother. Clearly, the overall role of learning at school in these areas is limited to formal knowledge and technical abilities, although there have been some good initiatives such as a 'Get Cooking' campaign to introduce children to the skills involved in preparing and cooking food. Knowledge acquired at school can be, and often is, reinforced by daily routines in the home.

• The above information is an extract from *Parent Power2– A Practical Guide to Children, Shopping and Advertisements* by the Food Advertising Unit at the the Advertising Association. See their web site at www.fau.org.uk or alternatively page 41 for their address details.

Why UK consumers are on a spending spree

By Lisa Bachelor

The fact that we're in the midst of a global recession, that jobs are being cut nationwide on a daily basis and that interest rates can't fall much further, doesn't seem to have distracted UK shoppers from hitting the high street in recent weeks.

Buoyant consumer spending, as well as an unexpectedly firm market in house prices, are the reasons behind the Bank of England's decision to hold interest rates this afternoon.

It seems consumers are the elbow propping up the UK economy, as the manufacturing and services sector show little improvement and job losses continue.

Part of the reason for such consumer confidence is down to the nation's 16.6m homeowners, who are feeling flush with cash after seven interest rate cuts this year have cut about £100 a month off a £60,000 mortgage.

With nearly 70% of UK property bought rather than rented, mortgage rates make a big difference to consumer spending, and the current mortgage rates akin to those last seen in the 1960s have left consumers feeling confident.

Following the September 11 attacks, consumers did initially shy away from the high street amid fears of a recession, which seemed partly confirmed by October data showing house price growth grinding to a halt.

However, last month the Bank of England cut rates by an unexpected 0.5%, house prices took another turn upwards and consumers headed back to the shops with the pressing thought of Christmas uppermost in their minds.

> **It seems consumers are the elbow propping up the UK economy, as the manufacturing and services sector show little improvement and job losses continue**

What is difficult to tell is how long the consumer will continue to prop up the economy once the usual flurry of spending around the festive season comes to an end.

Certainly consumers are set to spend more this Christmas than ever, with most of it going on credit cards, but this could be partly psychological as fears that the economy will suffer further next year could be resulting in a case of 'spend while you can'.

The New Year could well see such extravagant spending slow down as people gear up for a rocky ride, what with the likelihood of growing unemployment coupled with the post-Christmas hangover of mounting debts to pay off.

Certainly analysts seem divided on how the Bank of England will need to react next year.

'Consumer spending in particular is seasonally buoyed which may make the extent of the economic slowdown and the effect of the cuts to date hard to judge,' said Ian McCafferty, chief economic adviser at the Confederation of British Industry.

Much of the consumer spend in January is also at the mercy of the weather. An unusually warm winter so far has meant that the clothing sector has suffered as the usual rush for winter coats and hats has failed to take place.

Unless the frost sets in for the New Year, consumers may well choose to put their purses away and start squirreling rather than spending.

Children and advertising

The effect of advertising on children and the use of children in advertisements are sensitive issues. The British Codes of Advertising and Sales Promotion – the self-regulatory guidelines written by the advertising industry – include vital requirements in this area

The rules

When dealing with complaints about advertisements featuring or aimed at children, the ASA is guided by the following basic principle:

'Advertisements should contain nothing which is likely to result in physical, mental or moral harm to children, or to exploit their credulity, lack of experience or sense of loyalty.'

Advertising aimed at children

Today's consumer receives hundreds of advertising messages each day. Adults can view these with a sceptical eye, but children are more vulnerable. The Codes contain special rules for advertisers who target this group:

Pester power

A crucial requirement of the Codes is that advertisements targeting children should not actively encourage them to make a nuisance of themselves to parents or others. One magazine advertisement for a children's TV channel was criticised by the ASA for suggesting that children without access to it should complain to their parents

Easy to understand

Advertisers should clearly state the price of a product featured and should not exaggerate its appeal or performance. A toy, for instance, must not be shown to be larger than it really is. Complex issues should not be oversimplified: in 1998 complaints were upheld about an advertisement which implied that a diet involving breakfast cereal could help to stop overweight children being bullied.

Direct appeals

Goods which are considered too expensive for the majority of children to buy should not be advertised to children. An electronics firm advertising computer software at prices starting from £40 in a children's publication was criticised by the ASA; most children would not be able to afford them.

Nuisance

Advertisements should not actively encourage children to make a nuisance of themselves to their parents or others. Neither should they make children feel inferior or unpopular for not buying the advertised product. The ASA recently upheld a complaint against an advertisement which showed a grinning boy being scowled at enviously by two other boys, whose faces had been shaded green. The headline ran: 'Who's Got The New [Computer] then?'

Responsible

Advertisements should not encourage children to eat or drink at or near bedtime, to eat frequently throughout the day or to replace main meals with sweets and snacks.

Parental permission

Advertisements should make clear to children that they must obtain permission to buy complex or expensive products. For promotions where the prizes may cause a conflict between parent and child, consent is also required.

Advertising which features children

The safety of children is of paramount importance in advertisements. Advertisements must not, either by message or example, lead a child into a potentially dangerous situation. The Code details a number of specific requirements in this area. The general rule is that:

'Children should not be encouraged to copy any practice that might be unsafe for a child.'

Advertisements should not encourage children to talk to strangers or enter strange places. Children should not be depicted unattended in street scenes or shown playing in the road unless they are old enough to be responsible for their own safety. Likewise, they should always be seen to observe the Highway Code. Children should not be shown using or in close proximity to dangerous substances such as medicines or equipment such as electrical appliances, without direct adult supervision.

One advertiser who featured a sleeping baby in a cot on top of a washing machine to demonstrate its low noise levels was asked to withdraw the advertisement. The ASA also criticised a large supermarket for its leaflet entitled 'Streets Ahead for Children's Clothing' which showed a photograph of a child standing in a shopping trolley being pushed at speed by another.

Subject, context and choice of media

Advertisers would break the Codes if their approach was violent or capable of disturbing young readers. In judging such complaints, the Authority takes into account the context in which the advertisement appeared and the relevance of the advertisers' approach.

Facts and figures

Advertisers take their responsibilities very seriously when advertising to children or featuring them in their campaigns. In 1998 the ASA received 12,217 complaints; 212 concerned children of which 53 were upheld relating to 7 advertisements. This compares with 10,678 complaints received in 1997; 84 concerned children of which 6 were upheld relating to 2 advertisements.

• The above information is an extract from the Advertising Standards Authority's web site which can be found at www.asa.org.uk

© Advertising Standards Authority

Forget flying the flag. We're all global now

UK icons bite the dust as consumers shop in a world without frontiers

By John Arlidge

What could be more British than British Airways, Rover cars and Moss Bros? The answer, a major new study of Britain's consumer culture has revealed, is a wide range of top brands. The rapid explosion of consumer choice has left some of Britain's best-known names looking as outdated as warm beer and village greens.

Superbrands, an independent body that monitors Britain's changing tastes, will this week publish the first league table of the UK's strongest brands. Of the top 100 less than half are British. Once unshakeable icons, notably British Airways, Rolls-Royce, Barclays Bank, Littlewoods and Rover cars, have been forced out by foreign rivals.

The study reveals the dramatic changes in consumer tastes in the days since food meant meat and two veg, MFI was the last word in interior decoration and the only way to arrive was in a car with 'Made in GB' bolted to the bumper. Consumers are more outward-looking than ever and have helped Britain transform itself into the European capital for media, financial services, leisure and pleasure.

Superbrands, an independent group of image makers that has helped to create many of Britain's strongest brands including BT, Vodafone, Tesco and Virgin, collated sales figures, recognition surveys and wide-ranging market research to identify the top 100 brands offering consumers 'physical or emotional advantages which they recognise and for which they are willing to pay a premium'. The results provide a fascinating snapshot of our changing tastes.

Far from being 'little Englanders', consumers have developed a taste for all things European. Ikea, the Swedish furniture manufacturer, outshines Conran and Habitat. More

Britons drink Evian than English, Welsh or Scottish bottled water. We may not all look like David Ginola or Jennifer Aniston but we all think we are worth a little L'Oreal pampering and Nivea is our favourite face cream.

Alfa Romeo's recent renaissance has made the marque as desirable as Range Rover. We may be turning our backs on our own railway companies but the Eurostar makes it into the top 100 and Club Med outdoes British tour firms.

> ## Far from being 'little Englanders', consumers have developed a taste for all things European

Britain is a nation of technophiles, the survey shows. Almost two-thirds of us now own a mobile phone and more than half of those are models made in Finland by Nokia or by the Swedish firm Ericsson. BT makes it into the top 100 along with One2One and the £160 billion global telecoms giant, Vodafone.

Despite the recent collapse in confidence in internet firms, Britons are the most enthusiastic web surfers

in Europe. America Online is our favourite service provider, with more than 1 million members, and the burgeoning popularity of email has helped Microsoft's Hotmail win 'superbrand' status.

The travel sector is booming, creating new superbrands, which are outperforming established giants. British Airways failed to make it into the top 100 but Virgin Atlantic is praised as 'distinctive, fun-loving and innovative' and EasyJet, the low-budget Luton-based carrier, has become a new consumer champion, forcing down air fares.

The Superbrands study highlights the astonishing weakness of British manufacturing. The only large-scale British-based manufacturers to gain superbrand status are Land Rover and the electronics firm Psion.

The only compensation is that industrial decline has been partly offset by the rapid growth of the creative industries – media, financial services, fashion and food. Of the 45 British-based companies in the top 100, a remarkable 13 are food and drink firms, 10 provide media services from TV channels to the internet, eight sell financial services and two make clothes and shoes. The leading food firm is Prêt A Manger, the upmarket lunch chain, which has transformed the British sandwich from a national joke into something so good that the world's biggest fast-food company, McDonald's, has taken a £25 million bite out of the company.

Among financial services companies, Abbey National, Nationwide, First Direct, Britain's first telephone bank, Direct Line insurance, and Scottish Widows are the most trusted.

Twenty years ago the BBC accounted for two-thirds of all television programmes and even more radio. Deregulation and the advent of multi-channel digital television have led to the creation of new masters of the media universe. Sky has used Premier League and international football, pay-per-view film channels and Britain's first 24-hour rolling news service to win superbrand status just 10 years after its launch. It boasts 5 million digital viewers.

Channel 4, which went on air in 1982, also makes it into the top 100 following the success of its 'insightful and intelligent' comedies such as *Da Ali G Show, Friends, Frasier* and *Smack the Pony* and the channel's revamped coverage of English cricket.

The *Sun*, 'an emotive, humourous, passionate icon of contemporary culture', is Britain's only newspaper superbrand.

The top 100 contains some welcome news for companies that have suffered a sharp slump in profits or which have been embroiled in controversy. Marks & Spencer, Britain's biggest clothing retailer, remains a superbrand because it 'guarantees high quality and affordable prices'. The National Lottery has survived a bribery scandal, software glitches and the bitter battle between Camelot and Richard

Branson over who should run the game to remain the nation's favourite flutter.

Even though he suffered a rare defeat last year when his People's Lottery's bid was rejected by the Lottery Commission, Branson remains Britain's most powerful brand owner. The entrepreneur has shrugged off the recent poor performance of Virgin trains to make it into the top 100 twice with his music-to-mortgages Virgin group and Virgin Atlantic.

'We want the best and in the global market place it does not matter whether it is British or not'

Among the major losers is British Airways, which is still suffering from its disastrous 'ethnic tail-fin' rebranding and has dropped out of the top 100.

The spread of 'dress-down' casual wear and the growing popularity of Italian and American fashion designers such as Giorgio Armani, Gucci, Calvin Klein, Tommy Hilfiger and DKNY have forced out the starchy Moss Bros.

Parker pens, which once filled

every inside pocket, have been dumped in favour of PalmPilots and cheap disposable Biros. Hoover has lost out to British innovators such as James Dyson, inventor of the bagless vacuum cleaner.

The health craze has helped force out some 'sin brands', including Benson & Hedges cigarettes. Happiness is no longer a cigar called Hamlet.

Marcel Knobil, who chairs Superbrands, says the league table confirms that British consumers have 'undergone a transformation of attitude and style. From chip butties to microchips and macintoshes to iMacs, the British are no longer prepared to put up with the mediocrity that characterised so much of our past. These days we want quality, creativity, innovation and passion.

'We want the best and in the global market place it does not matter whether it is British or not. We are very happy to speak English on a Scandinavian telephone, using airtime bought from a British company, while we drink French water and eat a Thai chicken wrap in our Ikea kitchens.'

• The above article appeared in *The Observer* on 11 March 2001.

Interbrand/*Business Week* ranking of 40 of the world's most valuable brands

2001 Brand rank		2001 Brand Value ($MM)	% change	Country of origin	2001 Brand rank		2001 Brand Value ($MM)	% change	Country of origin
1	Coca-Cola	68,945	-5%	US	21	Honda	14,638	-4%	Japan
2	Microsoft	65,068	-7%	US	22	BMW	13,858	7%	Germany
3	IBM	52,752	-1%	US	23	Nescafe	13,250	-3%	Switzerland
4	GE	42,396	11%	US	24	Compaq	12,354	-15%	US
5	Nokia	35,035	-9%	Finland	25	Oracle	12,224	N/A	US
6	Intel	34,665	-11%	US	26	Budweiser	10,838	1%	US
7	Disney	32,591	-3%	US	27	Kodak	10,801	-9%	US
8	Ford	30,092	-17%	US	28	Merck	9,672	N/A	Germany
9	McDonald's	25,289	-9%	US	29	Nintendo	9,460	N/A	Japan
10	AT&T	22,828	-11%	US	30	Pfizer	8,951	N/A	US
11	Marlboro	22,053	0%	US	31	Gap	8,746	-6%	US
12	Mercedes	21,728	3%	Germany	32	Dell	8,269	-13%	US
13	Citibank	19,005	1%	US	33	Goldman Sachs	7,862	N/A	US
14	Toyota	18,579	-1%	Japan	34	Nike	7,589	-5%	US
15	Hewlett-Packard	17,983	-13%	US	35	Volkswagen	7,338	-6%	Germany
16	Cisco Systems	17,209	-14%	US	36	Ericsson	7,069	-9%	Sweden
17	American Express	16,919	5%	US	37	Heinz	7,062	N/A	US
18	Gillette	15,298	-12%	US	38	Louis Vuitton	7,053	2%	France
19	Merrill Lynch	15,015	N/A	US	39	Kellogg's	7,005	-5%	US
20	Sony	15,005	-9%	Japan	40	MTV	6,599	3%	US

Source: Interbrand

The way we live now

Too good to be true

By John Arlidge

Work is over and it's time to relax. You walk into a bar and overhear a group of fashionable types loudly ordering a new kind of Polish vodka. You order the same, with tonic. The barman tells you it's the bar's first birthday and the vodka is on the house.

The man next to you has walked out leaving behind a packet of white-filter cigarettes you've never seen before. You take one and go and sit down at a table next to two girls dressed in red who are both reading the same magazine. They smile at you. Outside a man is fly-posting images of a new car on a lamp-post.

Free booze, free fags, smiley girls, and edgy-looking types indulging in a little impromptu street art. It's your kind of place, it's your night, and for one seductive moment you actually feel you have joined the ranks of the officially cool. But have you? Take a closer look.

That loud group with the Evisu jeans are still ordering vodka, but none actually has a glass. The man who left his cigarettes behind is back at the bar with a newly opened packet, but he is not smoking. The girls in red are doing a lot of smiling, but very little reading and the man outside with the stickers is climbing into a new £40,000 BMW.

Whaaassssuup? You've been had. You are not a young urban funkateer everyone wants to know and buy a drink, you are the victim of the latest scam dreamt up by the advertising industry to seduce you – us – into buying more of this or that brand of drink, cigarette, magazine, car, clothes, or snack. Those perfectly ordinary, hip, happy-looking people in the bar are not your new best friends, they are the new secret agents of capitalism – 'brand ambassadors' paid by advertisers to look good and sell, sell, sell.

If you ask them, these diplomats of desire will, of course, deny all knowledge of their secret assignment. They have to sign a confidentiality agreement before they are told what they will be flogging, but do not be fooled by the blank looks. They are the shock troops of undercover marketing and this summer they are coming to a bar, club, pub or festival near you.

Viral marketing is spreading like the common cold as advertisers turn their back on the traditional hard sell in favour of street-level guerrilla campaigns. Young consumers, firms' top target, are becoming harder and harder to reach. They are promiscuous, hopping from this TV channel, to that DJ, to their favourite internet site, and they are discerning, switching off when over-paid, over-exposed actors and celebrities try to tell them what to do in flashy, expensive commercials. 'Below-the-line' stealth marketing, which creates word-of-mouth recommendation, is marketing's new Holy Grail.

Sean Pillot de Chenecey, the London-based trends forecasting consultant who works for Saatchi & Saatchi, Wieden & Kennedy and McCann Erickson, explains: 'Major brands – especially those targeting the key youth market – are having an absolute nightmare trying to cut through the ever-growing clutter of advertising, promotion and sponsorship that surrounds us. Firms know word of mouth remains the most effective form of advertising and they are using young brand ambassadors to take their advertising from the virtual world of TV, the internet or radio into the real world of clubs, bars, pubs, and even the home. It may not be considered ethical, but it's certainly effective.'

Real-life production placement agencies pay approachable, aspirational, pretty but not-too-good-looking-to-give-the-game-away types to wear the right clothes, drink the right drinks in the right places, drive the right cars, use the right words, listen to the right music, and eat the right snacks. They hope that people will notice, talk, tell their friends, who will then tell their friends, and their friends until they create an unmistakable 'buzz'.

Every type of firm is at it – from underground record labels to some of the world's biggest companies – Microsoft, Kelloggs, BMW, Apple.

It can happen almost anywhere and is gradually taking over the internet, the workplace, homelife and leisure time. 'We seem to be moving towards a sort of *Truman Show* situation where the world is full of "real people" acting as your best mates when, in fact, they are paid brand spokesmen,' De Chenecey says. 'In future you'll never be quite sure whether your neighbour is offering to lend you his lawnmower because he wants to help, or simply because he is a brand ambassador for Flymo.'

So next time you pop out to a bar after work and someone attractive offers to buy you a drink 'because we're celebrating', remember, they may not be as happy as they look.

After all, they're working. You're not. So be sure to enjoy a drink – at their expense – but don't forget to ask for the reality check on the way out.

• The above information appeared in *The Observer*, 12 August, 2001.
© *Guardian Newspapers Limited 2001*

> *Viral marketing is spreading like the common cold as advertisers turn their back on the traditional hard sell in favour of street-level guerrilla campaigns*

Richest 10% spend seven times more than poorest

By John Carvel

The gap between rich and poor was demonstrated yesterday by official figures showing that the 10% of households in the top income bracket spent nearly seven times as much as the 10% with the lowest incomes.

In an average week the richest 10th spent £849, including £187.50 on leisure items such as cinema, theatre, television, holidays, gambling and gardening. The poorest 10th spent £126.70, including £20.20 on leisure.

This latest slant on inequality in the UK came in the family expenditure survey for 2000-01 published yesterday by the office for national statistics.

It showed average household spending (excluding taxes, savings and purchase of capital goods) was £390 a week. The biggest outlay was on leisure, with households averaging just over £70 a week on spare-time activities, compared with £64 on housing, £62 on food and non-alcoholic drink and £55 on motoring.

Spending on leisure goods and services increased by 10% last year, accounting for 18% of household spending. Higher mortgage costs caused spending on housing to overtake food and drink as the second biggest item in the family budget.

The richest 10th of the population spent 12% more than the second richest 10th. Average weekly outgoings for the richest were: £145.80 on leisure services and £41.70 on leisure goods, £141.10 on housing, £118.30 on motoring, £111.40 on food and non-alcoholic drinks, £70.60 on household goods, £54.80 on household services, £45.80 on clothing and footwear, £33.80 on alcohol, £32.70 on personal goods and services, £28.20 on fares, £16.60 on fuel and power, £6.50 on tobacco and £1.60 on sundries.

Weekly outgoings for the poorest 10th were: £25.80 on food and non-alcoholic drinks, £21 on housing, £14.10 on leisure services and £6.10 on leisure goods, £11.20 on household goods, £8.60 on fuel and power, £8.60 on motoring, £8.50 on household services, £6.70 on clothing and footwear, £5 on personal goods and services, £4.20 on alcohol, £3.90 on tobacco, £2.70 on fares and 20p on sundries.

The ONS said the spending gap was slightly higher than 12 months before when the richest 10th averaged £782 a week and the poorest £120. But proportionately the gap was greater 10 years ago when the richest spent £513 and the poorest £69. The figures are not adjusted for inflation.

The survey showed average household spending in rural areas was higher than in all other parts of the country except London. In spite of the low incomes of many rural workers, average weekly spending was £420 a week, compared with £460 in the London built-up areas and £320 in small towns.

Spending was highest in London, the south and eastern region, and lowest in north-east England. Londoners spent 19% of their income on housing, 3% above the national average, while in Northern Ireland housing accounted for 10%.

Those living in the north-east spent the most on alcohol, averaging £16.50 a week, compared with a national average of £14.80.

The survey was based on information from 6,500 people through the UK who kept a two-week diary of outgoings.

Who has what:

- Of the poorest households 75% have a washing machine but only 4% a dishwasher, against 68% of highest income households
- Average weekly spending on mobile phones rose by 500% from 1995 to 1999 to £2, and to £2.10 in 2000/01, with fixed lines at £5.80
- Spending on clothing and footwear averaged £22 a week in 2000/01
- Spending on milk fell by 25% to £2.10 between 1995 and 2000/01

THE LEARNING CENTRE

Your rights as a consumer

Don't be a fool – know your rights as a consumer. Are you aware of your rights? Alison Steed reveals the results of a new survey

Many consumers are unaware of their rights, making them easy prey for Del-Boy style tricksters, a new survey has found.

The MORI poll, which was undertaken for the Department of Trade and Industry, showed that few of us actually know our rights as consumers, making us vulnerable to sharp practices and poor service.

But the new consumer minister, Melanie Johnson, has vowed to 'kit out' shoppers with a better understanding of their rights.

She said: 'Confident consumers get the best deals. Confident consumers want choice, quality and decent prices – this in turn drives product and service innovation so healthy competition needs consumers who are kitted out with an understanding of their rights.'

According to the survey, around 40 per cent of us don't know much about products or services before we buy them, with those over 55 least likely to know about products before purchasing. Most people, 85 per cent of us, do look for information before we buy goods, usually about the price.

However, just 18 per cent of those surveyed looked for information about money, savings and investment products before they bought them.

Despite this apparently reasonable amount of upfront checking, one in three of those surveyed still had cause to complain about goods and services in the preceding 12 months, but only a quarter of those surveyed knew that a retailer does not have the right to repair a faulty product before offering a refund.

Such complaints are dealt with by Trading Standards officers and Citizens' Advice Bureaux staff every day. Moira Haynes, of the National Association of Citizens' Advice Bureaux, said: 'The sort of things that we deal with are problems with faulty goods, credit agreement cancellations and problems with second hand cars. That is very much what the CAB service is all about.'

Around 40 per cent of us don't know much about products or services before we buy them, with those over 55 least likely to know about products before purchasing

---

According to the Office of Fair Trading's annual report for last year, the OFT dealt with 842,270 complaints in total last year, most of which related to house fittings and appliances. Home maintenance, repairs and improvements alone accounted for 70,736.

Alison Buchanan, of the Office of Fair Trading, said: 'A lot of people are confused about what to do if they have faulty goods. That is a common complaint that we hear about. We have a lot of people phoning up looking for advice. We support what Melanie Johnson is saying about kitting out consumers.'

The DTI launched Consumer Support Networks in October last year, with a £20 million grant over three years from the Treasury's Capital Modernisation Fund. The DTI said that the initiative aims to bring 'together existing services which are often fragmented'.

Ms Haynes said: 'We are part of the new Consumer Networks that are being set up. We support the initiative, and are playing a part in that by expanding our capacity to give consumer advice. You can go to our website Advice Guide to get information on consumers' rights.'

The OFT supplies a number of free leaflets on consumer rights, which can be obtained by phoning 0870 6060321, or emailing oft@echristian.co.uk

The DTI's information leaflet *Unsatisfactory Goods: Your Rights as a Consumer* can be obtained by calling 0870 1502 5000.

© Telegraph Group Limited, London 2001

Basic consumer rights

Millions are unaware of their basic rights says citizens advice

Millions of people do not know the full extent of their employment, benefits and consumer rights according to a new National Association of Citizens' Advice Bureaux (NACAB)/MORI survey launching in Advice Week September 3-10 2001.

NACAB/MORI asked a representative sample of 2,010 people a series of six questions concerning their basic rights and more than 56 per cent of respondents got more than three of the questions wrong. People were least likely to know the maximum they could be charged for NHS dental treatment but there was also confusion about the rate of the minimum wage, paid annual holiday entitlement, the minimum income level guaranteed to pensioners and their rights when returning faulty goods.

Only one person in the entire 2,000-person sample got all the questions right. Differences between regions varied on individual questions but people in London were most likely to get more than three questions wrong (see table).

NACAB chief executive David Harker said: 'People today need to know so much more about the numerous policies and regulations relating to their rights often just to claim what is rightfully theirs. This survey shows that, understandably, people don't immediately have all the necessary information to hand and explains why sources of information and advice such as the Citizens' Advice Bureau are so essential.'

Main findings from the survey show that:
- 42 per cent of people believe the national minimum wage to be higher than it actually is
- 75 per cent of people – including 75 per cent of those aged over 65 – do not know how much a single pensioner is entitled to under the government's Minimum Income Guarantee

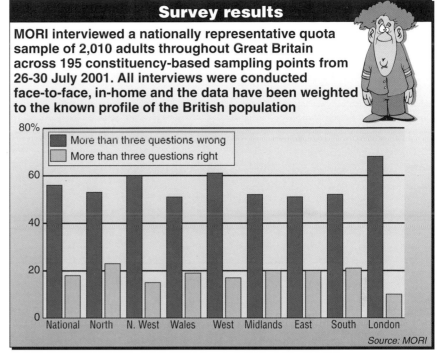

Survey results

MORI interviewed a nationally representative quota sample of 2,010 adults throughout Great Britain across 195 constituency-based sampling points from 26-30 July 2001. All interviews were conducted face-to-face, in-home and the data have been weighted to the known profile of the British population

Legend:
- More than three questions wrong
- More than three questions right

(Chart categories: National, North, N. West, Wales, West, Midlands, East, South, London)

Source: MORI

- Only 7 per cent knew the maximum amount that an NHS dentist can legally charge for a course of treatment
- 57 per cent were unaware that people in full-time employment are entitled to four weeks' paid annual holiday
- More than half – 51 per cent of people – were unaware that they are entitled to a full refund when purchased reconditioned second-hand goods turn out to be faulty
- Although 59 per cent of people correctly knew that non-payment of a TV licence can result in imprisonment, 8 per cent thought that they could be imprisoned for not paying their credit card bills

David Harker continued: 'One of the aims of the CAB service has always been to ensure that individuals do not suffer through lack of knowledge of their rights and responsibilities or of the services available to them. This is why we now offer specialist services and advice on virtually any subject in more places and in ways which respond to the needs of people in an increasingly busy and complex world.'

Information on the subjects covered in the survey and in general can be obtained via a local CAB, many CABs throughout the country now deliver advice in places like health centres, hospitals, courts and prisons, libraries and community centres or by accessing Adviceguide, NACAB's on-line information website.

For further information on the subjects dealt with in the NACAB/MORI Survey:
- For advice on the Minimum Income Guarantee contact the MIG telephone helpline for pensioners on 0800 028 1111.
- The Consumers' Association has published a series of 24 leaflets explaining people's legal rights on everything from welfare benefits and employment to problems with goods and services. These can be obtained from local bureaux, libraries and community centres or by calling the Legal Services Commission leaflet line on 0845 3000 343.
- Local Health Authorities hold lists of NHS dentists and can provide information on charging.

Their numbers can be found in local telephone directories.

- Each local authority will have a trading standards department, the next port of call after CABs concerning consumer rights. Their number can be found in the local telephone directory.

Notes

1. Citizens' Advice Bureaux deliver free, confidential, independent and impartial advice from over 2,000 outlets across England, Wales and Northern Ireland. Bureaux belong to the National Association of Citizens' Advice Bureaux (NACAB) which sets standards for advice, training, equal opportunities and accessibility. NACAB also co-ordinates national social policy, publicity and parliamentary work. NACAB and each CAB are registered charities and rely on the work of over 21,000 volunteers and almost 5,000 paid staff. Bureaux in Northern Ireland are supported by the Northern Ireland Association of Citizens' Advice Bureaux (NIACAB). Bureaux in Scotland belong to a separate organisation, Citizens' Advice Scotland.

2. Advice Week kicks off in London's Covent Garden on Monday 3rd September. Free CAB advice on any subject is being offered on board a branded double-decker Advice Week bus at Covent Garden's East Piazza on Monday 3rd September from 10am to 4pm. This event has been made possible through the support of the National House-Building Council.

- MORI interviewed a nationally representative quota sample of 2,010 adults throughout GB across 195 constituency-based sampling points from 26-30 July 2001. All interviews were conducted face-to-face, in-home and the data have been weighted to the known profile of the British population.

© MORI

General consumer rights

Information from the Office of Fair Trading (OFT)

Your statutory rights

There are certain basic legal rights you have when you buy goods or services. These rights apply to goods bought or hired from a shop, street market, mail order catalogue or doorstep seller. They include goods bought in sales.

And when you pay for service, the law entitles you to certain standards.

Buying goods

The law says that goods must be:

- of satisfactory quality – they must meet the standard that a reasonable person would regard as acceptable bearing in mind the way they were described, what they cost and any other relevant circumstances. This covers, for instance, the appearance and finish of the goods, their safety, and their durability. Goods must be free from defects, even minor ones, except when they have been brought to your attention by the seller, for example, if the goods are said to be shop-soiled;

- fit for their purposes, including any particular purpose mentioned by you to the seller – for example, if you are buying a computer game and you explain that you want one which can be played on a particular type of machine, the seller must not give you one that cannot;

- as described – on the package or a display sign, or by the seller. If you are told that a shirt is 100% cotton, then it should not turn out to be cotton and polyester.

These are your statutory rights. All goods bought or hired from a trader – whether from shops, street markets, mail order catalogues or door-to-door sellers – are covered by these rights. This includes goods bought in sales. When you decide to complain, bear in mind how the item was described. A new item must look new and unspoiled as well as work properly, but if the goods are secondhand, or seconds, then you cannot expect perfect quality.

Many traders have goodwill policies which go beyond your statutory rights. For example, some stores will allow you to exchange goods which are not faulty, such as clothes which are the wrong size.

If things go wrong

If there is something wrong with what you buy, tell the seller as soon as possible. If you are unable to return to the shop within a few days of making the purchase, it is a good idea to telephone to let it know about your complaint. Make a note of the conversation and to whom you spoke.

If you tell the seller promptly that the goods are faulty and you do not want them you should be able to get your money back. As long as you have not legally *accepted* the goods you can still *reject* them – that is, refuse to *accept* them. One of the ways you accept goods is by keeping them, without complaint, after you have had a reasonable time to examine them. What is reasonable is not fixed; it depends on all the circumstances. But normally you can

at least take your purchase home and try it out. If, however, you delay in examining what you have bought, or in telling the seller about a fault, then you may lose your right to reject.

Note that if you signed an acceptance note on receiving goods this does *not* mean you have signed away your right to reject. You still have a reasonable time to examine them. Letting the seller try to put faulty goods right also has no effect on your rights – if the repair fails, you still have any right to reject that you had when you agreed to the repair.

Once you have, in the legal sense, *accepted* goods, you lose your right to a full refund. You can only claim compensation, and you have to keep your claim to a reasonable minimum. Normally you have to accept an offer to put the goods right, or the cost of a repair. But if the goods are beyond economical repair you are entitled to a replacement, or the cash value of a replacement if none is offered.

Credit notes

When you reject faulty goods you may be offered a replacement, free repair or credit note. You do not have to agree to any such offer. You can insist on having your money back in full. If you accept a credit note you will not usually be able to exchange it for cash later on. So you may be left with an unwanted credit note if you cannot find anything else you like in the shop. Moreover, some credit notes may be valid for only a limited period.

Guarantees

Some goods have manufacturers' guarantees. These are useful when your statutory rights no longer apply. Claiming under guarantees often results in fewer quibbles than relying on your statutory rights, provided you complain within the guarantee period.

Do not be put off by traders trying to talk their way out of their responsibilities.

- The law says it is up to the seller to deal with complaints about defective goods or other failures to comply with your statutory rights. So do not accept the excuse that 'it's the manu-

facturer's fault'. But you may have additional rights against the manufacturer under a guarantee.

- You have the same rights when you buy sale goods as at any other time; the seller cannot get away with notices saying there are no refunds on sale goods. Think twice before you buy from a trader who displays a notice like this. It is against the law, and local authorities can prosecute the trader.
- You have the same rights even if you lose your receipt. A receipt, however, is useful evidence of where and when you bought the goods.
- You may be able to claim compensation if you suffer loss because of faulty goods; for example, if a faulty iron ruins your clothes.

Presents

If you received the faulty goods as a present, you may have to ask the person who bought them to complain for you, or to authorise you in writing

---

You have the same rights when you buy sale goods as at any other time; the seller cannot get away with notices saying there are no refunds on sale goods

---

to complain on his or her behalf. Only the buyer has the statutory rights described earlier.

Returning goods

You are not legally obliged to return faulty goods to the seller at your own expense. If an item is bulky and would be difficult or expensive to return to the shop, ask the seller to collect it. But this does not apply where you complain about faults after having *accepted* the goods, or if you got the goods as a present.

Private sales and auctions

You have fewer rights if you buy privately (that is, not from a trader) or at an auction. But if you are injured by defective goods, or they cause property damage costing you £275 or more, you have certain rights regardless of how they were bought or whether they were a gift. If in doubt seek further advice.

You have no real grounds for complaint if you:

- were told about the fault;
- examined the item when you bought it and should have seen the fault;
- did the damage yourself;
- made a mistake when purchasing the item;
- simply changed your mind about the item.

Under these circumstances you are not entitled to anything, but many shops will help out of goodwill. It is always worth asking.

Buying a service

When you pay for a service – for example, from a dry cleaner, travel agent, car repairer, hairdresser or builder – you are entitled to certain standards. A service should be carried out:

- with reasonable care and skill – a job should be done to a proper standard of workmanship. If you get a new extension to your house, the walls should not start to crack and the roof must not leak;
- within a reasonable time – even if you have not actually agreed a definite completion time with the supplier of the service;
- at a reasonable charge, if no price has been fixed in advance – if the price was fixed at the outset, or some other way of working out the charge was agreed, you cannot complain later that it is un- reasonable. Always ask a trader how much a particular job will cost. The trader may only be able to make an informed guess at the cost and give you an estimate. If you agree a fixed cost it is usually called a quotation. A fixed price is binding whatever it is called.

Where materials (such as bricks or wallpaper) are used in the provision of a service, or the service involves fitting goods (such as double-glazing or radiators), the materials and goods are covered by the same statutory rights as when you buy them directly.

Whether you are buying goods or services, it could be worth checking, before you part with your money, whether the business or person providing the service is a member of a trade association. Membership does not guarantee satisfactory work, but if anything goes wrong, it could make it easier to get things put right. In some sectors trade associations are very active and have codes of practice. If a trader does adhere to a code of practice this may also benefit you if a problem arises.

Unfair contract terms

You are not bound by a standard term in a contract with a trader if it unfairly weights the contract against you. This applies particularly to exclusion clauses. But a new law means that, in contracts concluded

---

If you believe you have bought unsafe goods, you should contact the trading standards department of your local authority

---

since 1 July 1995, other kinds of unfair small print are also covered. Examples include

- penalty clauses and (except in special circumstances) terms which give the trader the right to vary the terms of the contract (for instance, by increasing the price) without you having the right to withdraw;
- terms which try to stop you holding back any part of the price of goods or services if they turn out to be defective, or prevent you from withdrawing from the contract while allowing the trader to do so;
- terms which allow the trader to dishonour promises, for instance, ones made by salesmen; or
- terms which try to stop you being able to go to court over a dispute.

The new law applies to standard terms – those you have not negotiated yourself – in contracts for goods and services that you buy as a consumer. Terms that define what you get and how much you pay are not covered

unless they are unclear. So the law cannot be used to argue that a contract does not represent fair value for money.

It is for the courts to decide if a term is unfair. If you think a term is unfair and you do not wish to be bound by it, you may wish to seek advice from your local trading standards department or citizens' advice bureau. You can also write to the Director General of Fair Trading. When he receives a complaint about a term, if he considers it unfair he can take action in court to stop its use in future contracts. He cannot, however, get involved with individual cases.

Consumer safety

It is an offence for a supplier to sell goods unless they are safe. This applies to both new and secondhand products, but not to antiques or to goods needing repair or reconditioning, providing you were clearly informed of this fact. If you believe you have bought unsafe goods, you should contact the trading standards department of your local authority. Prompt action may help prevent accident or injury to other customers.

• The above information is an extract from the Office of Fair Trading's web site which can be found at www.oft.gov.uk

© Crown Copyright

I don't believe it!

Is the rise in consumer complaints legitimate or are we just a nation of moaning minnies?

When did you last make a complaint? Not a mini moan or a whingeing whimper but a full-blown assertive: 'I would like to speak to the manager' or 'This is not good enough'. A real Victor Meldrew blow-out.

Today's consumers won't just moan for Britain – apparently we can take on the rest of Europe as well. According to a report from Royal Mail, conducted by the Henley Centre, we are not just complaining more but doing so through a greater range of channels. People in the UK are more likely to voice complaints than their European counterparts by email, post or telephone. In the past year we managed to pick up the phone to 'out-moan' our continental counterparts by 37%. Needless to say, we are generally complaining far more. Over the past four years the percentage of UK complainers has reached 45%, says the report.

Just look at all those websites. A quick surf will bring up a myriad of sites devoted to airing ordinary folk's grievances. Don't suffer alone if you didn't get the response you wanted from the offending bank or company. Why not let the world share your gripes and post it on the web? So deliciously satisfying.

So why this complaining culture? Should TV programmes such as *Watchdog* and organisations such as the Consumers' Association take all the credit? 'People are that much better informed of their rights,' says Gareth Headon, spokesman at the CA. In addition, people in the workplace are ever keen to make sure they are not on the receiving end of shoddy services and bad business practice. Rather than putting up and shutting up, the trend is now to assert rather than acquiesce. There comes the time when the secretary or PA has to be, let's say, assertive in making their displeasure known.

By Wendy Smith

Sue Hyatt is PA to the managing director of Virgin Mobile Telecoms, Tom Alexander. If the conference centre or travel agent screws up, then it reflects badly on her, she says. Mind you, whatever the level of aggravation, Hyatt is a firm believer in maintaining her cool when registering her dissatisfaction. 'I don't think shouting gets you anywhere. The best thing, I find, is to play to people's better nature.'

People in the UK are more likely to voice complaints than their European counterparts by email, post or telephone

She also points out that people will respect you more if they know precisely what you will and won't accept. 'I feel that we do have a right to object and be honest when things are not correct.'

Hyatt once found her boss featured in the publicity blurb (photo and all) of a conference he had not even agreed to speak at. She had to make the objection but in such a way that they could all continue their working relationship in the future. 'We didn't want to fall out with the company, but I felt that they had to know they had overstepped the mark and I think they appreciated the honest approach,' she says.

So much for dishing out the honesty, what is it like working at the sharp end of receiving it? Customer relations manager for First Direct Bank, Annette Stilwell, has worked with irate people for the past seven years. And she has noticed the changes. 'People know they have the right to complain and they will go right to the top, and they are that much more aggressive.'

Her advice for the best way to make a complaint is to: write down all the points you want to talk about; remain calm; keep a diary of who you have spoken to and on what day; treat people you are speaking to with respect and build a rapport with the person at the end of the phone. However, if you are still not satisfied with the person dealing with you – they may not have had adequate training – ask to speak to a supervisor.

So is complaining worth the hassle? Are we seeing the required results? Or is it just an opportunity to get things off your chest and let off steam? According to CA research, just over half of all complaints are successfully resolved. 'Half may be successful but what about the other half? We need to keep up the complaints as we still have a long way to go,' says Headon.

Shops in the wrong over your rights

Many stores have failed to answer the call to clean up their act over extended warranties. And, to add insult to injury, sales staff seem to have no idea what consumers are entitled to by law

By Mary O'Hara

Seven years after the Office of Fair Trading first declared that extended warranties on electrical goods were overpriced, and that some retailers were employing questionable sales tactics to sell them, it has launched a 'thorough' investigation to find out if things have improved.

The results of mystery shopping exercises, carried out at more than 200 retailers across the country, has convinced the OFT that self-regulation by the British Retail Consortium (BRC) – introduced after the initial investigation – may not be working.

A similar shopping exercise by *Jobs & Money* appears to reinforce this view. Not one of the assistants at the retailers we looked at seemed fully aware of the rights of consumers when it came to repair of goods. And, overall, the quality of information supplied by sales people was patchy and far from accurate.

We found huge variations in the cost of warranties – some charge up to £250 for four years' extended cover on a £500 TV for example, while others such as House of Fraser, Debenhams and John Lewis were offering free five-year extended warranties for similar products.

Shop assistants were only vaguely aware of what their competitors were offering, and none could demonstrate that their policies were better value than taking out a multi-appliance policy through an independent insurance company. And all, bar one, claimed the cost of repairing goods yourself would be more expensive.

Staff seemed unaware of general consumer rights provided by the Sale of Goods Act 1979. The Act says that when you buy goods from a trader they must fit the description, be of satisfactory quality – which includes lasting a reasonable length of time – and be fit for their purpose. If the goods are not of satisfactory quality, you are entitled to compensation which is normally the cost of repairs. The retailer, not the manufacturer, is legally obliged to sort out a problem if the goods don't meet these requirements.

> *Retailers have been lambasted over the years by consumer groups who say shoppers have long been the victims of over-zealous sales people pushing extended warranties*

A manufacturer's one-year guarantee is in addition to these rights – many of whom offer free repair or replacement without dispute.

Retailers are quick to point out that a manufacturer's guarantee fails to include accidental damage, but this does not necessarily mean a warranty is value for money if you can take out independent accidental cover for less.

Under the Act, retailers are responsible for faulty goods (that is, not of 'satisfactory quality') for up to six years – or five in Scotland – after purchase. What is deemed a 'reasonable' product life expectancy does determine whether the item qualifies, but if a TV is bought for £500, it would be 'reasonably' expected to work for many years.

The problem with the law is that, should you run into problems, it could be expensive to pursue a claim.

Retailers have been lambasted over the years by consumer groups who say shoppers have long been the victims of over-zealous sales people pushing extended warranties. They say the OFT's action is not a moment too soon.

'Seven years is a long time to take action, from when the OFT first highlighted extended warranties as a problem,' the Consumers'

Association says. 'We have said for years that on domestic products, extended warranties are often a waste of money.'

A much-touted benefit of extended warranties is 'peace of mind' and is often the primary reason for people taking one out. But the fear of breakdown far exceeds the likelihood of it happening, and even if a breakdown occurs, there is little evidence to suggest that should you pay to have it fixed yourself, it will cost more than a warranty.

Research carried out by the Consumers' Association in April last year found that the average repair bill for a washing machine, for example, was £43. To justify a warranty on an average washing machine (between £150-£200 over four years), it would need to break down three times. Yet only 3% of washing machines suffer this many breakdowns.

Extended warranties are a £1bn business – up from £650m in 1994. The OFT says the cost of individual warranties may have decreased since then, but its new investigation is 'necessary to establish the current picture'.

'It is important for consumers to be aware that not everyone signs up to the BRC voluntary code and they should check before buying something,' a spokesman said.

'There is evidence of high-pressure selling. We want to see if they offer value for money and to see if there is transparency of information and if there is sufficient competition. Two-thirds of retailers don't adequately advertise the price of their policies, for instance.'

The latest investigation, to be conducted by the newly established Markets and Policy Initiatives Division of the OFT, could take up to a year to complete.

Retailers, especially those who have signed up to the voluntary code, say the way warranties are sold and the value they offer has improved dramatically.

Dixons, for example, which signed up to the code as soon as it was set up, spends hundreds of thousands of pounds each year training staff and has recently launched a number of multi-appliance warranties 'to offer consumers greater choice'.

It says: 'Our staff go through rigorous training and we do our own mystery shopping to see how policies are sold. Staff are instructed to mention the warranties at the point of sale, but in no way should they put pressure on people to buy. We think our policy offers great value for money. People wouldn't buy them if they didn't think they were good value for money.'

The results of the new OFT investigation may bring some pleasant surprises. But in the meantime, consumers would be well advised to consider all the options – including not buying a warranty at all.

Before you say yes

- Always ask: 'Do I really need this warranty?' and 'Do I really need to buy it now?'
- Even if you believe the retailer's warranty is the best deal on offer, take time out and buy it later. Compare the price and the level of cover with independent policies or look into multi-appliance policies.
- Many retailers offer to match the price of electrical goods if you can find them cheaper elsewhere – usually within 28 days – so check if you can get the items and/or warranty cheaper elsewhere within the time frame allowed.
- Always read the exclusions and small print carefully – however much of it there is.
- Check out your home insurance policy to avoid any duplication.

Consumer wrongs

You may know now when a consumer is right but do you know when a consumer is wrong? Look at these problems:

I bought these trainers half an hour ago for £60 and I've seen them in another shop for £40
- I haven't worn them and they are still in the box
- I've got my receipt
- The shop has to give me my money back when I ask for it
- That is right, isn't it?
Wrong!

I bought a shirt yesterday but now I don't like the colour
- I haven't worn it
- I've got my receipt
- The shop has to give me my money back this time, doesn't it?
Wrong!

Sorry, but you never have the right to ask for a refund if there is nothing wrong with the goods.

Remember that you have a contract with the shop and this gives you responsibilities.

It does not give you the right to change your mind after you have bought something, whatever the reason.

All you can do is go back to the place where you bought it with your receipt and ask really nicely for a refund.

If you are lucky they will say yes but legally they do not have to.

Smart shoppers know that shops like to help them when things go wrong and that it's not always the shop's fault when problems happen.

• The above information is an extract from the Trading Standards Institute's (TSI) web site which can be found at www.tradingstandards.gov.uk

How to complain

Information from the Office of Fair Trading

Complaining about goods

Go back to the shop as soon as possible. If you have the receipt or other proof of purchase, take this with you. Explain the problem, say what you want done, and set a deadline.

If you are not satisfied, put your complaint in writing. If the shop is part of a chain, write to the head office. Address your letter to the customer services manager or the chairman.

If none of this works, get further advice, or consider whether you want to take the matter further by going to court.

Complaining about services

'Consider getting a written expert opinion to back up your complaint'
Complain to the supplier, giving it a chance to put the matter right. If you are not satisfied, put your complaint in writing, saying what you want done, and set a deadline. If you are dealing with a larger business, address your letter to the customer services manager or the chairman.

Consider withholding any further money until the problem has been sorted out, but check the small print of any contract you have signed. It may be desirable to seek further advice.

Be especially careful about withholding payments if you have a credit agreement. You may wish to take advice on this. If you stop paying it could affect your credit rating and so your chance of getting credit in the future. Continuing to pay will not undermine any claim you have against the lender for unsatisfactory service by a supplier.

Keep copies of letters along with a diary of events and a note of any telephone calls. Take photographs if relevant.

Consider getting a written expert opinion to back up your complaint. The motoring organisations can, for example, provide reports on cars, but any reputable

trader with relevant experience can count as an expert. This may cost money, but could be invaluable if you need to take legal action.

If you did not fix a price and you think you have been overcharged when the bill arrives, get quotes from other traders for comparison when you complain. Some may charge to provide a quote.

If you have a problem with goods or services bought on credit, you may have some additional protection.

General tips

If you telephone:
1. make a note beforehand of what you want to say;
2. have receipts and any other documents handy;
3. get the name of the person you speak to;
4. write down the date and time and what is said;
5. follow up your call with a letter, particularly if your complaint is a serious one.

If you put it in writing:
1. describe the item or service;
2. say where and when you bought the item or when the service was done, and how much it cost;
3. explain what is wrong, any action you have already taken, to whom you spoke and what happened;
4. say what you want done to remedy

the situation – for example, a refund or repair, or the job done again without charge;
5. consider using special delivery so that you can easily check whether your letter has been delivered;
6. keep copies of any letters you send. Do not send original documents, such as receipts and guarantees – send copies instead.

Who can help?

If you cannot seem to get anywhere with your complaint or you need some extra advice, the following organisations may be able to help you:

Trading standards (or consumer protection) departments
They can help in many situations relating to goods and services. They have powers to investigate complaints about false or misleading descriptions or prices, inaccurate weights and measures, consumer credit and (except in Northern Ireland) the safety of consumer goods. They will often advise on everyday shopping problems. The address is in the telephone book under your county, metropolitan district, London borough or Scottish regional council. In Northern Ireland contact the trading standards branch of the Department of Economic Development.

Some trading standards departments run consumer advice centres near main shopping areas. These offer advice and information to shoppers and traders, and deal with problems and complaints.

Environmental health departments

These deal with health matters such as unfit food and drink, dirty shops and restaurants, and, in Northern Ireland, consumer safety matters. The address can be found in the telephone book under your district, metropolitan district, London borough, Scottish district or Northern Ireland borough council.

Citizens' advice bureaux

They can help with a wide variety of problems, including shopping complaints. Look under Citizens' Advice Bureaux in the telephone book.

Law centres

These are place where you can get free advice from qualified lawyers. It is worth checking if there is one near you.

Trade associations

Traders often belong to trade associations. Some of these have codes of practice, and some have low-cost conciliation or arbitration schemes. A code of practice is not legally binding, but it can be a guide as to whether traders have broken rules by which they claim to abide. If they have, then an arbitrator should find in your favour. Not everyone who claims to be a member of a trade association is, so it is worth checking with the association. You can find the names and addresses of relevant trade associations from your local library or citizens' advice bureau.

Utilities

If you have a complaint about utilities (gas, water, electricity, or telephones), try first to sort out the problem with the company. Your bill will have a customer service telephone number that you can call. These four utilities each have a regulator who has the power to help resolve consumers' problems.

Ombudsmen

There are ombudsmen for services such as banking, building societies, funerals and insurance.

• The above information is from the Office of Fair Trading's web site which can be found at www.oft.gov.uk

Alternatively, see page 41 for their address details.

Would you credit it?

Young people have cash, and the new generation of online retailers are after it. But without a credit card, just how do you buy on the internet? As the dust settles on the nation's annual consumerfest, PJ White looks into the issues behind the new technology that is letting young surfers e-shop till they drop

The commercial logic is irresistible. Young people have spending power – an estimated £30 billion a year in the UK. They have grown up familiar with the internet. Chat rooms, e-mailing and websites are environments as comfortable to them as they are worrisome to older generations.

So they will have none of the resistance to online shopping that their parents had. There is nothing that cannot be made available for sale over the internet. Especially easy are teenage interest goods such as clothes, cosmetics, cds, computer games and videos. That all adds up to a potentially profitable seam. And e-retailers are very keen to exploit it.

Until recently, there was a major stumbling block: methods of payments. Under-18s cannot have credit cards, and credit cards are the conventional way of purchasing online.

Step in new forms of payment, such as Splash Plastic and Smartcred.

Simple pre-pay systems, they are modelled on the solution to the same problem with mobile phones.

Until recently, there was a major stumbling block: methods of payments. Under-18s cannot have credit cards, and credit cards are the conventional way of purchasing online

---

This is how they work. You visit the card company's web site and apply for a card. A week later it arrives in the post along with a pin number. It looks like a credit card, but isn't. You revisit the web site and activate it. Then you take it to a high street shop that participates in the scheme,

along with some cash. Give your card to the shop assistant, with the cash you want to spend on the net and ask for a top up. The shop assistant swipes your card, and loads your account. Typically, you have to put in at least £5, with a daily maximum of £250.

You then shop on the internet. When you get to the check-out, you select your card as your payment method, and enter your username and pin. Your account is debited and the goods are despatched.

You can't spend more than is loaded on your card. When you start to run out of gas, you get pumped up again, just as you load airtime on a mobile phone.

With payment barriers out of the way, the race is now on to get young people signed up and spending. Retailers, or at least those in the business of hyping them, are drooling over the potential as the arithmetical logic unfolds. There are 3.7 million 12 to 16-year-olds in the UK, and around 1.5 million internet users under 17. Teenagers aged 12 to 17 represent 12 per cent of the European online population. In the US and Europe, they are forecast to spend $1.3 billion online this year.

Is this a welcome prospect for young people? Is it liberating or exploitative?

The pro-arguments are that young people learn to budget – they have to stay within the spending limit. They are spending their own cash, not borrowing parental credit cards. They practise the skills they need to become savvy consumers, comparing prices and finding bargains. They have a much wider choice. Rural young people are compensated for their isolation – they can acquire the newest designer gear as fast as city kids.

On the debit side are fears of exploitation. Here is simply another pressure for young people to spend, another form that retailers have found for aggressively targeting young people with things they don't particularly want or need but can be persuaded into. It ups the consumerist ante, widening the divide between the haves and have-nots.

It is also a solitary activity – rather than the more social habit of high street shopping – which is not necessarily what young people need.

One of the particular dangers goes with any form of virtual payment. Nottingham Trent University psychologist Dr Mark Griffiths calls it suspension of judgement. 'What we know about virtual payment is that it lowers the psychological value of money. People tend to spend more with debit and credit cards, because it is not like paying for things with real cash.'

That's why casinos and gaming machines work on chips and tokens. Subtle it isn't. You are more inclined to spend the tokens because you don't feel it is real money. In-store cards, encouraged by all major chains, ride on the same psychological mechanism. And young people are no less vulnerable, possibly more vulnerable, to it than adults.

Dr Griffiths has researched a lot about adolescent gambling, and is concerned about the ease with which various forms of plastic cash permit online gambling. This involves not just the newcomers but cards such as Solo, a conventional debit card like the better known Switch but for 13 to 17-year-olds. 'There is nothing really to stop them being used with internet gambling sites', says Mark Griffiths.

'What we know about virtual payment is that it lowers the psychological value of money. People tend to spend more with debit and credit cards, because it is not like paying for things with real cash'

Hard gambling is one thing, shopping another. Dr Griffiths recognises six classic components of addiction that can be applied to any behaviour. For online shopping to be an addiction it would have to be the most important thing in the person's life. They would build up tolerance – needing more to get the same effect – and it would modify their mood, giving a buzz or a high or being a way to escape from worries. Addicts get withdrawal symptoms if they cannot indulge the habit, experience conflicts, say with relationships or other activities, and have a tendency to relapse to square one if they start again after giving up.

These are behaviours youth workers might look out for – though there is little sign that it will be a major problem for young people. 'People can do things to excess – but excess is not addiction,' Dr Griffiths says.

• Two of the leading companies enabling young people to buy online without credit cards are: www.splashplastic.com and www.smartcreds.co.uk

• The above information is an extract from *Young People Now* produced by the National Youth Agency (NYA). *Young People Now* is the leading monthly magazine for everyone working with young people. Every month it offers news, listings, reviews and in-depth features on issues of concern and special interest. There are also regular pages on health and activity, global issues, politics and power and briefings from the NYA's database youthinformation.com. *Young People Now* is essential reading for youth workers, those in the Connexions Service, health advisers, PSHE teachers and others working in informal education with young people. Published monthly – 12 issues. Annual subscription £22.80 – single copies £2.00 – discounts for bulk orders available on request. See page 41 for their address details or visit their web site at www.nya.org.uk

© *National Youth Agency (NYA)*

Participation[1] in gambling activities

Men are more likely than women both to gamble and to participate in a greater number of gambling activities. Bingo is the only gambling activity in which women are more likely than men to participate. Gambling is most popular with people aged 25 to 54.

Great Britain							Percentages
	16-24	25-34	35-44	45-54	55-64	65-74	75+
National Lottery Draw	52	71	72	72	69	61	45
Scratchcards	36	32	23	17	16	11	6
Fruit machines	32	22	15	8	6	3	1
Horse races	12	19	15	14	11	9	5
Private bets	21	18	11	10	6	5	3
Football pools	4	9	8	11	13	10	6
Another lottery	8	9	8	9	9	8	6
Bingo	7	7	7	6	7	9	10
Dog races	6	7	4	4	2	1	1
Other betting with a bookmaker[2]	5	5	63	2	2	1	-
Table games in a casino	4	5	3	2	1	-	-
Any gambling	66	78	77	78	74	66	52

1 Respondents aged 16 and over who said that they had participated in gambling in the past year.
2 Betting other than on horse or dog racing

Source: British Gambling Prevalence Survey, National Centre for Social Research

Limits to your rights

Information from the Office of Fair Trading (OFT)

There are limits to your statutory rights. For example:
You have no legal grounds for complaint if you:
- were told the fault;
- examined the item when you bought it and should have seen the fault;
- did the damage yourself;
- made a mistake when purchasing the item;
- simply changed your mind about the item.

Nevertheless, to win customer goodwill, many shops will be helpful if you have proof of purchase. It's always worth asking.

Special types of transaction
Your rights may vary in certain situations:
- Private sales
- Auctions
- Secondhand goods
- Faulty presents

Private sales
- You have fewer rights when buying privately, through an ad in a local newspaper for example, so the golden rule is 'buyer beware'.
- Privately bought goods do not have to be free of faults but must be as described. For example, a leather coat should not be plastic and a motorbike should have 12 months' MOT if advertised as such.
- Although you should be able to take legal action if the seller misleads you about the condition of the goods, it is better to go prepared. Take someone with you to act as a witness or ask for a written description of the goods.

Traders who pose as private sellers
Traders who pose as private sellers are trying to take advantage of your limited rights and this is illegal. Be wary if the seller:
- has lots of small advertisements with the same telephone number in a local paper.

- insists on meeting you at your home.

If you've purchased faulty goods from a suspected trader contact your local trading standards department. If the person is a trader your full statutory rights will apply and the trading standards department can take action to stop the individual misleading the public.

Auctions
Take care if you buy at an auction.
- Auctioneers can refuse to accept responsibility for the quality of the goods they auction.
- Look out for exclusion clauses and read notices and catalogues carefully.
- Note any conditions of sale, such as buyers' premium, terms and method of payment, deposits, and time limits for removal of goods.
- You cannot back out of the deal once the hammer has fallen.

Secondhand goods
You have the same rights when buying secondhand as when buying new goods. You can claim your money back or the cost of repairs if goods sold to you are faulty provided:

- the faults are not due to wear and tear to be expected when second-hand;
- were not pointed out to you;
- were not obvious when you agreed to buy the goods.

Faulty presents
Since statutory rights only apply to the buyer, if you receive a faulty item as a present, you may have to ask the person who purchased it to complain for you, or to authorise you in writing to complain on his or her behalf.

Sale goods
You have the same rights when you buy sale goods as at any other time. Beware of traders who display notices that say 'no refunds on sale goods'. These are illegal and local authorities can prosecute the trader. They are a type of exclusion clause which traders try to use to limit their responsibilities.

• The above information is an extract from the Office of Fair Trading's student web site which can be found at www.oftclp.com

Types of fraud

Information from Card Watch

Criminals use various methods of card fraud. Two-thirds of fraud on UK cards happens in the UK and the rest occurs overseas. Most of the fraud that takes place abroad is in the United States (22 per cent of losses on UK cards used abroad), Spain (16 per cent) and France (15 per cent). Fraud committed abroad on UK cards increased by 79 per cent in 2000 on the previous year's figure, costing £97.2 million.

Two major factors lie behind the increase. UK fraud prevention initiatives have driven criminals abroad; and criminals are increasingly moving quickly and easily from country to country. The Association for Payment Clearing Services (APACS) and its member banks and building societies are continuing to work closely with Visa and Europay/MasterCard on cross-border fraud initiatives.

The types of fraud used by card criminals are listed below:

Counterfeit fraud

Counterfeit card fraud cost almost £102.8 million in 2000, an increase of 104 per cent on losses of £50.3 million in 1999.

A counterfeit card is either one that has been printed, embossed or encoded without permission from the issuer, or one which has been validly issued then altered or re-coded.

Most cases of counterfeit fraud involve 'skimming', a process where the genuine data in the magnetic stripe on one card is electronically copied onto another, without the first cardholder's knowledge. In 1996 skimming accounted for 20 per cent of counterfeit fraud to amount to almost £3 million in losses. In 2000 card criminals are increasingly organised and as a result the proportion has grown to over 72 per cent to cost £74 million.

Skimming normally occurs at retail outlets – particularly restaurants and petrol stations –

where a corrupt employee copies a customer's card details before handing it back, and then sells the information on higher up the criminal ladder where counterfeit copies are made. Often the cardholder is unaware of the fraud until a statement arrives showing purchases they did not make.

It is vital that cardholders check their statements for any unfamiliar transactions

Fraud on phone, mail order or Internet transactions

Card-not-present fraud occurs when neither the card nor its holder is present at the point of sale, as happens in telephone, fax, mail order or Internet transactions. Most of this fraud occurs through telephone or mail order, and less frequently through the Internet.

This crime involves using fraudulently obtained card details to make a purchase. Usually the details

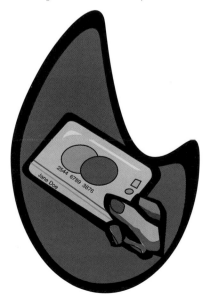

are copied down without the cardholder's knowledge or taken from discarded receipts. Less commonly, card details have been sourced from programmes which generate account numbers that have been set up on overseas Internet sites for short periods of time. As with counterfeit fraud, the legitimate cardholder may not be aware of the fraud until a statement is received.

A new address and card security code checking system to fight card-not-present fraud is being rolled out in the UK from April 2001.

Do not discard receipts carelessly and check statements for any unfamiliar transactions

Lost or stolen cards

Fraud on lost or stolen cards cost £98.9 million in 2000, an increase of 24 per cent on 1999's losses of £79.7 million. Most fraud on lost or stolen cards takes place at retail outlets before the cardholder has reported the loss. Card issuers are continuing to address this by using intelligent fraud detection systems.

A 'hot card file' system is used to distribute data about lost or stolen cards to 80,000 retailers in the UK to alert them to cards reported missing.

It is vital that cardholders report missing cards to their issuing bank immediately so a block can be put on the card

Mail non-receipt fraud

The number of plastic cards stolen in the post peaked in 1991 when it cost the industry £33 million and represented just under 20 per cent of total fraud losses. At this point the banking industry formed an ongoing partnership with the Royal Mail to monitor and control card distribution and this has driven the cost of mail non-receipt fraud down to £17.3 million in 2000.

Application fraud

Application fraud – using stolen or fake ID or other details to open a card account – was reduced by 11 per cent from 1999 to 2000, when it cost £10.2 million. The success in reducing this type of fraud is due to the use of CIFAS – The UK Fraud Avoidance System and other detection systems that help spot fraudulent applications.

ATM fraud

The majority of cases of ATM fraud occur when the legitimate cardholder has written down their PIN and kept it with their card in a purse or wallet which is stolen.

Some cases also occur through 'shoulder surfing' – where criminals look over a cash machine user's shoulder to watch them enter their PIN, then steal the card using distraction techniques or pickpocketing. ATM fraud cost the industry £17.9 million in 2000, 6 per cent of total fraud losses.

Never write down your PIN and be alert when using cash machines

• For further information about Card Watch phone 020 7711 6356 or email cardwatch@apacs.org.uk.

• The above information is an extract from Card Watch's web site which can be found at www.cardwatch.org.uk Alternatively, see page 41 for their address details.

© Card Watch

Top tips

Plastic card crime cost the UK almost £300 million in 2000 – but the financial loss is just part of the story

Being without the use of your plastic cards, for however short a time, can be extremely inconvenient. Just as important are the other personal items that can go missing when cards are stolen, such as house or car keys, driving licences, diaries, address books, family photographs, and other valuables.

A criminal can quickly spend hundreds or even thousands of pounds using your card or its details – often before you are aware that anything is amiss. More worryingly, funds from plastic card fraud may be used to support organised crime such as drug trafficking.

To help protect yourself from becoming a victim of card fraud, Card Watch suggests you follow these top tips:

• Guard your card.
• Don't let it out of your sight when making a transaction.
• Don't carelessly discard receipts from transactions.
• Check your receipts against your statements carefully. If you find an unfamiliar transaction contact your card issuer immediately.
• Never write down your Personal Identification Number (PIN) and never disclose it to anyone, even if they claim to be from your card issuer or the police.
• When using a cash machine, be wary of anyone who might be trying to watch you enter your PIN and do not allow yourself to be distracted by anyone trying to

talk to you.
• Report lost or stolen cards to your card issuer immediately. The 24-hour emergency number is on your last statement or call directory enquiries on 192.

Other important tips . . .
• Sign any new cards as soon as they arrive. Ensure that you cut up the old cards as soon as the new ones become valid.

• Don't keep you cheque book with your cards.
• If you carry a bag, carry it firmly with the clasp towards you. A money belt or secure inside pocket is best for valuables.
• Don't leave cards unattended in a bag, briefcase or jacket pocket in a public place and keep your bag or briefcase on your lap.
• At work keep your bag and other personal belongings locked in a cupboard or drawer.

• The above information is from Card Watch's web site which can be found at www.cardwatch.org.uk Alternatively, see page 41 for their address details.

© Card Watch

Dealing with credit

Credit can be a tempting way to shop but there are lots of possible snags if you lose control. It can be useful when making a necessary major purchase but if you get in too deep, you could end up with major money problems

Think carefully when using your credit card. Companies make money out of loaning you money you don't actually have.

How credit cards work

- Firstly, it's worth shopping around for a credit card. Some have annual fees while others don't. Interest rates vary too. So one card could prove much less costly to use than another.
- When you receive a credit card you'll be given a spending limit which you shouldn't exceed, and a minimum repayment which you must make every month.
- If you pay back everything by the due date shown on your statement, you can get up to 56 days' free credit.
- If you spend and pay back gradually you're charged interest. Compare the APR figure before choosing a card.
- APR (Annual Percentage Rate of charge). This is a standard measurement showing how good a deal the loan is. It includes most of the charges you have to pay. Usually, the lower the APR, the better the deal. If the charges included in the APR can vary, the interest rate and your repayments can go up or down. If your budget is tight you might be better off with a fixed-rate loan so that you know exactly how much you will pay each month.

Do you really need a credit card?

Plus side:
- Instant credit – buy now and settle up later.
- Short-term interest-free credit if you settle up in full.
- Spread the cost of big purchases, like a computer.

Minus side:
- It's easy to lose track of what

you've spent – lots of small purchases can really add up.
- You can pay through the nose until you've paid off the amount outstanding.
- You can get in big trouble if you don't keep up the minimum repayment.
- The temptation to spend money you haven't got can be hard to resist.

Extra protection when you use a credit card

- Using a card for a purchase can give you extra protection. For example, if you buy a new hi-fi and it doesn't work properly, you can claim against the card company if the shop doesn't put things right or has gone out of business.
- This applies to goods or services costing more than £100 for one item (but less than £30,000), even if you have only used your card to pay a deposit.
- Section 75 of the Consumer Credit Act 1974 says you have the right to claim against the credit card issuer in these circumstances. Further advice can also be obtained from your local trading standards department or Citizens' Advice Bureau.
- You do not have the same protection if you pay by a debit or charge card.

Insurance

You're not obliged to take insurance to cover credit card purchases. If you want insurance, check the terms of the policy carefully – some don't cover students for example.

On-line bandits

There's always a risk when shopping over the internet (or over the phone), or using credit cards in general. For example, when a restaurant bill is paid and the credit card is taken away for checking.

Some web sites offer a separate telephone service for making payments or establishing a contract. Other sites offer you the option of sending your credit card details via a secure (encrypted) page.

Remember though, this only protects your card details in transit. As with any other credit card purchase, the security of your card details ultimately lies in the hands of the retailer.

The OFT has published a web site of information and advice when buying over the internet.

If you lose your card

Keep your card safe. If it is lost or stolen, you must report it immediately. Your liability will then be limited to the first £50 that someone else spends. If you lend your card to someone and they go on a spending spree without your permission, you will be liable for everything they spend before you report it.

Consumer Credit Research Group

Everything you ever wanted to know about plastic cards, especially credit cards. CCRG is a lobbying and promotion body funded by the credit and debit card industry.

- The above information is an extract from the Office of Fair Trading's student web site which can be found at www.ofthelp.com

© 2000 Crown Copyright

Ways to pay

There are many ways to pay. Do you know which is best for you?

Cash/money

Cash is simple to control. You can see it and touch it and when you spend it you can see that the amount of cash that you have is getting smaller and smaller.

When you have spent all of your cash you can't spend any more.

But carrying large amounts of cash is not safe. If it is lost or stolen it is probably gone for ever.

Cheques

Cheques come in a cheque book and are supplied by your bank.

Your money is kept in a bank account and when you want to buy something you just write a cheque out and give it to the shopkeeper. The money is then taken out of your account and given to the shop.

Cheques are safer than cash because they can only be used to take money out of your account if they are signed by you.

You will need a special card to use with your cheques. It will show how much you can spend with each cheque.

But you must keep a record of your cheques so that you know how much you have spent and how much is left in your account.

If you spend more money than you have in your account, you will probably have to pay bank charges and interest.

Debit cards

Debit cards are beginning to take the place of cheques. These save you the trouble of writing out cheques – you just hand your card to the shopkeeper.

Then just sign the slip he or she gives you (after you have checked that the amount printed on it is correct).

The bank then takes the amount you have spent out of your account and gives it to the shop.

Credit

You might have heard of 'buy now, pay later'. This is the idea behind credit.

If you want to buy something expensive – a CD player for example – but haven't got enough money, it is sometimes possible to borrow the money and pay it back over a period of time.

You can borrow money from a bank (this is called a bank loan) or you can borrow it from a shop (where you will sign a credit agreement – a type of contract).

You get the CD player fairly quickly and just pay a little of the money back each month.

Sounds easy doesn't it – but there may be problems:

1. If you can't afford the money now, how do you know that you will be

---

Never sign a credit agreement unless you are really clear about what it says and you are sure you can afford to pay

---

able to find the amount demanded every month?

2. If you borrow money you will almost certainly pay interest. This can be a great amount and the price of your CD player may double by the time you have paid for it. It may seem unfair but this is how banks and loan companies make their money.

3. Credit is easy to use but very difficult to get out of. The salesman in the shop may convince you that it is easy to pay but if you can't pay back all of the money you will be in debt – and that's a serious problem.

Never sign a credit agreement unless you are really clear about what it says and you are sure you can afford to pay.

If you are not sure about the agreement always remember that you can ask your family or friends, the Citizens' Advice Bureau or Trading Standards Department for help and advice.

Who owes all the money?

Information from the Consumer Credit Counselling Service (CCCS)

Contrary to the common perception of the young as reckless spenders, racking up credit like it's going out of fashion, new research from the Consumer Credit Counselling Service, sponsored by the Halifax, suggests it's 25 to 59-year-olds that are most likely to suffer from financial difficulties. Indeed, you are more likely to owe more than you can afford if you are Scottish, buying a home, aged between 25 and 39 and have a monthly income of between £500 and £1000.

The major new report, *When Credit Turns to Debt*, published by the Consumer Credit Counselling Service, identifies the profile of those most likely to suffer from what they term 'debt stress'. This refers not only to an individual's level of debt but also their debt-to-monthly-income ratio, the number of creditors they owe to and the likelihood of their approaching the CCCS for help in managing these difficulties.

The study of more than 10,000 people contacting the CCCS with multiple debt difficulties offers an invaluable insight into who gets into debt and should help address current Government concerns about over-indebtedness.

Broadly speaking, debt stress is associated with age, with nearly 60 per cent of all inquiries to the CCCS coming from a fifteen-year age band (25-39), and a further 30 per cent from the 40-59 age bracket. This offers some support to the life-cycle model of consumption, whereby individuals try to maximise utility over a lifetime within some anticipated income constraint.

Along gender lines, it is single males and couples that run up the largest debts. Median debt among female inquirers is £9,431, compared with £13,183 among men and £17,720 among couples.

Another key difference is between people buying homes and those who rent. While renters have an average debt-income ratio of 17.21 and owner-occupiers owe 17.98 times their monthly net income, the corresponding figure for homebuyers is 18.34.

Particularly striking is the median debt-income ratio of 44.27 for homebuyers with monthly net income below £500. Such debt is likely to be due to an unexpected fall in earnings, since such a low income would not normally secure a mortgage.

The report also considers regional differences and finds people in Scotland, the North-West, the West Midlands and the South-West to be most debt-stressed, while those in Northern Ireland, the South-East and London appear relatively less so. Median debt-income ratios of 14.67 and 14.73 in Scotland and the West Midlands compare with 11.92 and 13.41 in Northern Ireland and London.

Major findings of report

Over 90 per cent of people approaching the CCCS for help are aged between 25 and 59

Single women in general have smaller debts than either single men or couples

Low-income homebuyers appear to be most affected by debt stress, recording a median debt-income ratio of 44.27.

People with low-to-medium incomes are more likely to approach the CCCS for help than are those in deep poverty and the better-off.

People in Scotland, the North-West, the West Midlands and the South-West record the highest levels of debt stress.

Life-cycle model

Young earners over-consume now, deferring payment in the belief that their income will rise.

Nestmakers and new families approach their average lifetime earnings but make considerable outlays on consumer durables and homes and therefore borrow heavily.

Mature families are at the peak of their earning and can concentrate on clearing remaining debts.

The retired draw down saving for current consumption rather than obtaining further credit.

Notes

The CCCS offers free in-depth advice, debt management plans and

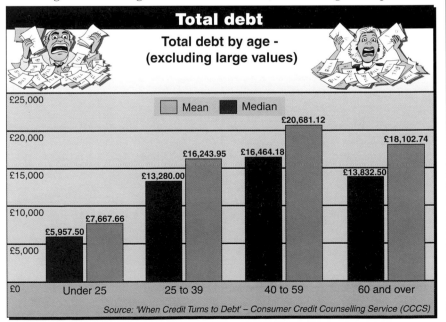

Total debt

Total debt by age - (excluding large values)

	Mean	Median
Under 25	£5,957.50	£7,667.66
25 to 39	£13,280.00	£16,243.95
40 to 59	£16,464.18	£20,681.12
60 and over	£13,832.50	£18,102.74

Source: 'When Credit Turns to Debt' – Consumer Credit Counselling Service (CCCS)

self-help packs to people in debt, supporting over 60,000 callers in 2000. Credit counselling is funded by voluntary donations by banks and other creditors. The level of donations is buoyant because, although counsellors put their client's interests first, creditors appreciate the efficiency of credit counselling and its sensitive handling of their customers in trouble. Freephone helpline: 0800 138 1111

Halifax is the UK's leading mortgage lender with around 2.5 million mortgages and a 19% market share. During 2000 Halifax achieved record mortgage sales of £19 billion. It is also a leading provider of credit cards.

With over 20 million customers, Halifax has a relationship with two in five households in the UK.

The Halifax's sponsorship of the CCCS's research is just one example of its commitment to encourage the provision of high quality debt counselling and money advice programmes across the UK.

• The above information is from the Consumer Credit Counselling Service's web site which can be found at www.cccs.co.uk Alternatively, see page 41 for their address details.

© *Consumer Credit Counselling Service (CCCS)*

Credit and debt

Information from the Office of Fair Trading (OFT)

Getting credit and staying out of debt

Buying on credit can bring its own problems, but it can give you extra rights too.

Sometimes it's not always easy to get credit or the credit deals that are available are less than generous. It is as important to shop around for credit as for any other purchase.

There's no easy way out of debt, but the sooner you face up to the problem, the easier it will be to solve.

Buying on credit

Most people at some time will use credit to purchase goods or services, for example, by obtaining a personal loan through a bank or building society, hire purchase, or a credit agreement with a trader. Before buying anything on credit you should consider the following points.

- Work out what the total cost of the loan will be.
- Shop around for credit: how much will a loan cost to repay each month and for how long? Check also the annual percentage rate of charge (normally referred to as APR). Generally speaking, the lower the APR the better the deal. Some traders offer interest-free credit (0% APR) but you will need to take care that you are not paying higher amounts in other ways; for example, it may be a higher cash price than you would pay for the same goods elsewhere.
- Make absolutely sure you have read and understood all credit agreements before signing them. If there is anything you do not understand, ask.
- Make sure you can afford to pay back the loan and the interest – and still have enough to cover all your other commitments.
- Check whether the loan has a variable rate of interest. If it has, your repayments can go up as well as down. Make sure you can really afford it.

Some loans are only given if they are secured on your home. These are not available if you rent. A secured loan gives security to the lender, not to you. If you cannot keep up with the repayments the lender can sell your home to cover any loss. You might get a lower rate of interest with a secured loan but you could have a lot at stake.

Your credit reference

No one has a right to credit. Before giving you credit, lenders – such as banks, loan companies and shops – want to check whether you are an acceptable risk. To help them do this, they may check with firms called credit reference agencies to get some details about you and your credit record.

The main credit reference agencies keep information on their computers about almost every adult in the UK

The main credit reference agencies keep information on their computers about almost every adult in the UK.

These agencies do not keep *blacklists* or give any opinion about whether or not you should be given credit. They simply provide information about your credit record. The credit reference agency will not be able to tell you why you were refused credit. It is the lender who decides whether you are an acceptable risk.

Credit reference agencies

The two main agencies in the UK are:
Experian Ltd, PO Box 8000, Nottingham, NG1 5GX. Tel 0115 934 4050.
Equifax Europe, Dept 1E, PO Box 3001, Glasgow G81 2DT. Tel 0990 783783

Your rights

If you are refused credit you have certain rights. In particular you have the right:

- to know the name and address of the credit reference agency that the lender contacted for details about you;
- to see any information held about you by that agency;
- to correct any inaccurate information.

The Office of the Data Protection Commissioner has responsibility for credit reference agencies and produces a leaflet, *No Credit?*, on how to consult your credit record

and correct any mistakes. You can order copies of it by phoning 0870 44 21 211.

Credit scoring

Many lenders use credit scoring systems which allocate points to various pieces of information given on your application form, such as your age, your occupation and whether you own your home. These points are added together to produce your credit score. This helps the lender predict whether you are an acceptable risk. Different lenders have different systems and *pass marks*, so you can be turned down by one but accepted by another. Your credit score is *not* part of the file kept on you by the credit reference agencies. Lenders do not have to tell you exactly why they have turned you down, but they should give an indication of the reason.

Cancelling a credit agreement

'If you can cancel, act quickly, as there are tight time limits'

You have a short time in which to change your mind if all the following points apply.

- You signed the credit agreement after discussing the deal face to face with the trader.
- You signed away from the contractor's or lender's premises.
- The amount of credit is between £50 and £25,000 and is not secured on your property.

When you sign, you should be given a copy of the credit agreement, which sets out your cancellation rights. You should also receive, by post, a second copy or a notice of your cancellation rights.

You cannot normally use these rights to cancel purchases made with a credit card because you will have entered the agreement for the card some time ago.

Withdrawing from an agreement

The effects of withdrawing are the same as cancelling

You can withdraw from any agreement before it has been signed by both you and the lender. This means acting quickly. If you have already signed, you will have to let the lender know that you have changed your mind before they sign. It's probably best to phone, fax or e-mail and then confirm by post. The effects of withdrawing are the same as cancelling.

This is particularly important with agreements secured on your home where the lender must send you an advance copy of the agreement at least seven days before sending the actual agreement to be signed. The lender must not contact you during this *consideration period* to give you time to think about the deal (but you can contact them).

Credit brokers' fees

If you use a broker to get a loan, including a mortgage or a loan

---

Even if you aren't up to your neck in debt, it's surprising how quickly it can build up and how long it takes to pay back

---

secured on your home, you will probably be charged a fee for the service. Make sure you know what this will be before you commit yourself. If, however, you do not enter into a loan agreement within six months of being introduced to a possible lender, the broker can only charge a fee or commission of £5 and if you have already paid more you can recover the excess. Similarly, other fees, such as a survey fee paid to the credit broker in connection with a loan that you do not eventually take up, are also refundable if you are borrowing £25,000 or less.

Extra protection when using credit

Buying on credit does give you some extra rights, for example, if goods are faulty. If a trader has an arrangement with a finance or credit card company to allow you to pay by credit, you have extra protection. This applies if the goods cost more than £100 but less than £30,000 including VAT. The credit company is equally liable for a breach of contract or misrepresentation by the trader. For example, if the goods are not delivered or are not what you ordered, or a holiday was wrongly described or you did not get what you paid for, you may be able to claim from the credit card or finance company.

Settling up early

You may find that part-way through repaying your loan, you have enough money to pay off the whole amount owing in one go. If so, you could be entitled to a rebate of some of the charges you would have paid over the rest of the life of the loan. It depends on the type of agreement you have with the lender. It can sometimes cost more than you expect to settle up early and in a few cases you could still have to pay more than the original amount borrowed. Even so, settling early will cost less than carrying on with the repayments plus interest for the full length of the loan.

Getting out of debt

'The sooner you face any debt problem, the easier it will be to solve it'

The sooner you face any debt problem, the easier it will be to solve it. Don't ignore it and hope it will go away. If you do, you could end up in court, lose the goods you've bought or find it difficult to get credit in future. You might even lose your home. Even if you aren't up to your neck in debt, it's surprising how quickly it can build up and how long it takes to pay back.

Work out exactly how much you owe, who you owe it to and what you can pay back. This will help sort things out in your mind, and help your creditors to see where you stand. Contact the creditor(s) as soon as possible to explain the problem and try to come to some agreement about repayments. Your debt won't be written off but you might be able to pay it back in smaller payments over a longer period of time. This will probably cost you more in interest payments in the long term but may be more manageable now.

Follow a five-point action plan:
1. How much do you owe? List your debts. Work out when payments fall. Identify the priority debts.
2. How much do you earn? Work out how much money you have coming in. Are you claiming all the benefits you are entitled to? Are you paying too much tax?
3. What do you spend? List your essential and less essential spending. Compare it with your incomings. What do you have left over to offer to creditors?
4. Nothing left over? Are there any areas in which you can cut down your spending? Is there any way in which you could earn extra money?
5. Talk to your creditors. Send them a financial statement showing your income and outgoings. Explain your offer to pay off your debt.

• The above information is from the Office of Fair Trading's web site which can be found at www.oft.gov.uk Alternatively, see page 41 for their address details.

© Crown Copyright

Seeking help with debt

This information applies to England, Wales and Scotland

Dealing with debt

It is usually possible to resolve a debt problem if action is taken early.

Some debt problems need to be dealt with urgently. A person may, for example, be faced with:
• gas or electricity disconnection
• court action for possession of her/his house
• bankruptcy, having received a notice called a statutory demand
• imprisonment for non-payment of a fine, maintenance, child support or, in England and Wales, council tax.

Often, a person with one debt that has become urgent will have other debts. It is important that all debts are looked at the same time because, when trying to sort out the debts, it is important that creditors know the person's full financial details.

What a creditor can do

A creditor who is pressurising someone for payment may not be aware of that person's financial circumstances. If the creditor is told about the circumstances and that the person is getting money advice s/he may agree to accept reduced payments or no payments at all. Although creditors are allowed to send reminders to a person who is in debt, they are *not* allowed to harass someone.

Dealing with a debt problem

If you have debt problems you should consult an experienced adviser, for example, at a Citizens' Advice

Bureau. Debt problems can be complex and many issues have to be taken into account.

Seeking advice

What to do first

Before seeing an adviser for debt, a person should gather all the papers which relate to her/his finances. These should include any court papers and letters, bills and credit agreements and details of her/his income.

If a person has to wait for an appointment it may be useful for her/him to tell creditors that s/he has contacted an adviser for help.

Most creditors welcome the involvement of a specialist adviser. They may be willing to hold off action to enable an agreement to be reached.

Helpful organisations

Citizens' Advice Bureaux

Citizens' Advice Bureaux are able to deal with money advice and debt problems. If it is a very complicated case they will usually be able to refer the person to a money advice specialist. This may be a solicitor or insolvency practitioner.

Money Advice Centres and Law Centres

Help is also available from Money Advice Centres or Law Centres.

The addresses and telephone numbers of local CABs, Money Advice Centres and Law Centres can be found in the telephone directory.

Money Advice Association

The Money Advice Association can also give details of the nearest adviser for people living in England and Wales. The telephone number is: 01476 594970.

Money Advice Scotland

Money Advice Scotland can give details of the nearest adviser for people living in Scotland. The telephone number is: 0141 572 0237.

National Debt Line

The National Debt Line can give free information to people living in England and Wales. It also provides an information pack dealing with debt.

The line is available on Monday and Thursday from 10 to 4 and on Tuesday and Wednesday from 10 to

7. The National Debtline telephone number is: 0808 808 4000.

If advice is not available when you need it

If someone with a debt cannot get help from a specialist organisation and is trying to solve the problem her/himself, s/he should:

- work out her/his net income and outgoings to see how much is left to pay off the debts
- deal with priority debts first. These are debts which, if unpaid, have serious repercussions – see under heading Dealing with debt
- get in touch with the creditors straight away to see if they would be prepared to accept smaller payments over a longer period
- check whether s/he is claiming all the benefits and tax relief s/he may be entitled to.

In England and Wales, there are also some factsheets that you may

---

Before seeing an adviser for debt, a person should gather all the papers which relate to her/his finances

---

find useful which have been produced by the National Association of Citizens' Advice Bureau (NACAB). They are available on the Citizens' Advice Line for London (CALL) web site. The address is http://www.cabline.org.uk/factsf.html

You should seek advice before borrowing to pay off debts, for example from a Citizens' Advice Bureau.

This is because these loans are usually very expensive. They could also be secured against your home which you could lose if you are not able to make the repayments.

If you are not sure how to proceed you should seek advice from an experienced adviser, for example from a Citizens' Advice Bureau.

- The information on the Adviceguide web site is produced by the Citizens' Advice Bureau Service. This information is checked regularly and incorporates changes made up to 1 January 2002.

- The above information is from the National Citizens' Advice Bureaux's advice guide web site which can be found at www.adviceguide.org.uk Alternatively, see page 41 for their address details.

© National Association of Citizens' Advice Bureaux

Preventing fraud

Information from Card Watch

As society's reliance on cards becomes more widespread, the losses from card fraud grow too. So while the rate of fraud growth as a percentage of turnover remains low – less than half the 1991 peak level of 0.33 per cent – it is vital that fraud prevention methods are continually developed and reviewed as criminals try to evade them.

Chip cards
Greatly increased security for payment cards
The banking industry's £300 million roll-out of 'smart' chip cards to fight card crime has become more crucial than ever with losses at an all-time

high. The new technology began to be rolled out in the spring of 1999, with each card issuer distributing the new cards in accordance with its own business plan, typically as old cards expire.

A chip card can be recognised by the gold-coloured contact plate on the front of the card, which contains a microchip with highly-

secure memory and processing capabilities. The cardholder can use them in exactly the same way as existing credit, debit and ATM cards.

Chip cards will still have a magnetic stripe on the back for a number of years to ensure that cards with old and new technologies can continue to be used throughout the UK as well as abroad.

The personal data held in a chip card is no different from that held on the existing magnetic-stripe card and covers such things as cardholder name, card number, expiry date etc. The information is simply held more securely to safeguard against counterfeit.

International use

To ensure chip cards are recognised and accepted in all countries where cards payments are made, countries around the world are building them to an international specification set by the international card schemes Europay, MasterCard and Visa (EMV).

The UK is at the forefront of an international roll-out of EMV-compliant chip technology. By the end of 2002 most of the bank-owned infrastructure in the UK will be processing chip cards and it is hoped that the upgrade of retailer-owned equipment will also be progressed rapidly. Upgrading systems quickly is vital to fight the steeply-rising rate of counterfeit fraud.

Benefits of chip cards

Initially, the major advantage is increased security against counterfeit fraud: a rapidly growing crime in the UK and around the world. Chip technology uses highly sophisticated processing to identify genuine cards and make counterfeiting much more difficult – and hugely expensive – for the criminal.

The new cards have the ability to support 'add on' services such as retailer loyalty schemes or electronic purse. Chip cards also have the potential to be used with chip readers attached to personal computers, mobile phones or digital TVs, making on-line transactions of the future even more secure.

With the increase in security that chip cards bring, the potential exists for retailers to expand the use of unattended terminals in petrol stations, telephone kiosks, car parks and self-scanning at supermarkets.

Identifying cardholders

A new way of identifying cardholders at the sales counter?

Chip technology provides a strong foundation for adopting a better method of identifying cardholders at the point of sale. Using this technology, the banking and retail industries are assessing the use of PINs (personal identification numbers).

Using an improved method of identifying the cardholder combined with the chip's ability to verify the

card is authentic would drastically improve security and significantly reduce most types of fraud.

If PINs are introduced to the retail point-of-sale environment, it will impact the UK's 42 million cardholders and necessitate a change in their behaviour at some 735,000 retail terminals. The massive scale of such a project emphasises the need for the banking industry, card schemes and retailers to work in partnership to ensure success.

Why not photo cards?

Putting identification photos on cards has been considered as an additional security method, but this would only provide costly short to medium-term relief. The banking industry aims to shift the responsibility of identifying the cardholder away from point-of-sale staff by relying on technology-based methods to help prevent fraud.

What about identification methods like iris scanning?

The memory capacity of the chip card makes it possible to retain biometric details for identifying the cardholder. Finger and iris scanning and voice recognition have all been promoted as possibilities, however such technology is not sufficiently reliable or cost effective to meet the requirements of the UK card industry within the next ten years.

System to fight fraud on phone, mail order and internet transactions

To combat the rapid rise in card-not-present fraud seen in the last few years, the UK card industry has developed a system that will be implemented by the international card schemes – MasterCard, Visa and American Express – from April 2001.

The automated system will allow merchants who accept transactions via the phone, mail order or the Internet to verify the billing address of a cardholder and cross-check a card security code. Cardholders will be asked to provide their full statement address and the last three or four digit number – known as the Card Security Code – printed on or just below the signature panel.

The system will have a significant impact as in the majority of cases, where a fraudster only has access to a receipt containing card details, they would not be able to provide the real cardholder's address and the code on the back of the card.

These checks will provide additional information to the merchant to help them assess the potential fraud risks and decide whether to proceed with the transaction.

The new system will reduce and deter this fraud type, while also helping to open up business opportunities for retailers. The system will initially be provided to the more fraud-prone card-not-present retailers, where transactions will be monitored to assess the system's effectiveness.

Knowledge-based systems

Checking for unusual spending patterns to spot fraud before it is reported

Banks, building societies and card schemes are continually increasing the sophistication of intelligent detection systems which can identify fraudulent transactions before a card's loss is reported. The majority of card issuers already use knowledge-based systems and have had considerable success in identifying spending patterns which differ from the cardholder's normal routine.

CIFAS – the UK Fraud Avoidance System
Sharing information to stop fraud
CIFAS is an information exchange that helps its wide range of member organisations identify different types of fraud, including that relating to false applications for plastic cards.

Lower floor limits
Online checks to ensure cards have not been reported lost or stolen
Most retail outlets have a floor limit – an amount above which they will seek authorisation from the card issuer before completing a transaction. Retailers have been encouraged to introduce lower floor limits since the early 1990s and the number of authorised transactions has increased from around 10 per cent to around 65 per cent.

These days the majority of fraud is authorised because criminals are using cards fraudulently before the owner reports it. This highlights the importance of cardholders reporting lost or stolen cards immediately so they can be blocked, and of checking statements regularly to look for any unrecognised transactions which could indicate card-not-present or counterfeit fraud.

The Industry Hot Card File (IHCF)
Checking every card transaction for lost and stolen cards
Retailers subscribe to this electronic file which distributes data on lost or stolen cards. When a card is swiped as part of a normal transaction, it is automatically checked against the file and an alert is given if the card's details match those on file.

The IHCF contains information on five million missing cards and is used by more than 80,000 participating retailers in the UK. During 2000 some 280,000 cases of attempted fraud were prevented using the system. The payments industry is actively encouraging

---

> **These days the majority of fraud is authorised because criminals are using cards fraudulently before the owner reports it**

---

extension of its use both in the UK and abroad, where it will help to combat cross-border fraud.

Helping retailers fight fraud
Training and then rewarding retail staff for stopping fraud
A major new retailer-training initiative, run on behalf of the UK banking industry in close collaboration with retailers, police and other organisations including Crimestoppers, is educating retail staff about how to identify and prevent card fraud attempts.

The Spot & Stop Card Fraud programme is targeting retailers in the top eight fraud-prone areas that account for around 40 per cent of all UK-based fraud (currently London, Manchester, Birmingham, Leicester, Glasgow, Edinburgh, Leeds and Croydon).

This initiative is part of a wider, ongoing retailer-education programme which includes producing a range of free publications and raising fraud-prevention awareness through initiatives like a Card Security Week held each September.

UK card issuers run a retailer-reward scheme which paid out more than £10 million in 2000 to staff who retained cards that were being used fraudulently.

Working with the police
Exchanging information to fight fraud
Working with the police is essential in fighting card fraud, particularly the organised criminals largely to blame for the UK's surge in plastic-card fraud.

Organised criminals often use sophisticated methods of card crime as a comparatively low-risk way of raising revenue that later funds more violent crime. Criminals behind offences like drug trafficking, kidnapping, smuggling and terrorism are often also involved in card crime.

Sharing information through the Fraud Intelligence Bureau (FIB)
The FIB based at APACS shares information and intelligence between the banking industry and police to combat counterfeit skimming. It has helped destroy several major counterfeiting rings run by organised criminals.

The FIB is further developing its role as a leading centre for exchange of information and intelligence between police and the banks on all types of card fraud.

APACS also provides speakers for police training courses as well as education materials. At an operational level, the banks and building societies liaise with the cheque and credit card squads regarding criminal activity and specific investigations.

> 'Organised criminals often use sophisticated methods of card crime as a comparatively low-risk way of raising revenue that later funds more violent crime. The penalties for card criminals are generally substantially lower than, for example, drug dealers.'
> David Cooper, Chairman of the Plastic Fraud Prevention Forum

For further information about Card Watch phone 020 7711 6356 or email cardwatch@apacs.org.uk.

• The above information is from Card Watch's web site which can be found at www.cardwatch.org.uk Alternatively, see page 41 for their address details.

Internet shopping

Information from Card Watch

The growth of e-commerce is explosive and people have voiced concerns about Internet security. So do cardholders need to be concerned? Card security relies upon vigilance and if cardholders follow some simple guidelines for making Internet transactions, it is no different from using the phone or mail order.

Card Watch recommends the following ten-point checklist to ensure security when shopping on the Internet.

1. Make sure your browser is set to the highest level of security notification and monitoring. The safety options are not always activated by default when you install your computer.

2. Two of the most popular browsers are Microsoft Internet Explorer and Netscape Navigator. Check that you are using a recent version – you can usually download the latest version from these browsers' websites. If you have a different browser or use on-line services such as AOL or Compuserve, contact your ISP or software supplier to find out how to activate their security features.

3. Keep a record of the retailer's contact details, including a street address and a non-mobile phone number. Beware if these details

are not available on the website. Do not rely on the e-mail address alone.

4. Click on the security icon to see if the retailer has an encryption certificate. This should explain the type and extent of security and encryption it uses. Only use companies that have an encryption certificate and use secure transaction technology.

5. If you have any queries or concerns, telephone the company before giving them your card details to reassure yourself that they are legitimate.

6. Print out your order and consider keeping copies of the retailer's terms and conditions and returns policy. Be aware that there may well be additional charges such as postage and VAT, particularly if you are purchasing goods from traders abroad. When buying from overseas always err on the side of caution and remember that it may be difficult to seek redress if problems arise.

7. Check statements from your bank or card issuer carefully as soon as you receive them. Raise any discrepancies with the retailer concerned in the first instance. If you find any transaction on your statement that you are certain you did not make, contact your card issuer immediately.

8. Ensure that you are fully aware of any payment commitments you are entering into, including whether you are instructing a single payment or a series of payments.

9. Never disclose your card's PIN to anyone, including people claiming to be from your bank or the police, and NEVER write it down or send it over the Internet.

10. If you have any doubts about giving your card details, find another method of payment.

Further information about e-shopping is available by visiting the Department of Trade and Industry's Consumer Gateway site at www.consumer.gov.uk

• The above information is from Card Watch's web site which can be found at www.cardwatch.org.uk Alternatively, see page 41 for their address details.

© Card Watch

Young, single – and £15,000 in the red

Which is more dangerous – a trip to the high street, or a quick spree in cyberspace? Barbara Oaff on women in a web of debt

Julie turned 18 last year. She quickly armed herself with several credit cards. She admits she then went 'completely mad' with her new buying power. That's no exaggeration. A week before Julie turned 19 she had amassed debts totalling £35,000.

Julie is not alone. Young women may be particularly vulnerable to a downturn in the economy because many are already struggling. Up to a quarter of them owe more than £15,000, a survey by women's magazine *Company* reveals.

It found that 75 per cent of women aged between 18 and 28 have some sort of debt. Of the 1,000 questioned, one in 26 said their bills were continuing to grow. Fifteen per cent owed between £5,000 and £10,000, and 30 per cent owed between £1,000 and £5,000.

The problem often begins at university, says *Company*, when young women build up student loans, overdrafts and credit cards, which they have difficulty managing when they have to pay high rents and support hectic social lives on low incomes.

But some independent financial advisers believe that internet shopping is partly to blame.

Kim North, an adviser with the Pretty Technical Partnership in London, agrees that the web has become one of the modern triggers of debt for young women. 'It is just so easy for them to spend, spend, spend 24-seven.'

Certainly, compared to the drudgery of Saturday shopping in the high street – getting into town, finding a parking place, dodging the rain, coping with the weekend crowds, dealing with stroppy shop assistants, and just trudging from one place to the next – shopping at websites is a doddle. Sites are quick to find, simple to navigate and easy to flick between.

And the depersonalised, disembodied nature of internet shopping makes a transaction seem almost unreal. Online buyers don't touch anything except their mouse and keyboard. They don't handle the goods. There is no handing over of real cash, and no need even to sign Switch or Visa chits. Nothing seems tangible.

For 29-year-old Nicola, this unreality was part of the pleasure of internet shopping. But it soon turned into the pain of debt. It wasn't long before she'd managed to point and click her way into a £30,000-plus deficit. Nicola started out quite shy of online shopping but soon overcame her inhibitions. She began to enjoy herself, not fully realising the impact of her actions on her future.

'You just start putting things into a shopping basket and you really don't realise how much you are spending. Because I wasn't physically holding anything I was buying, it was almost as if it wasn't real.'

But why women, and why the young ones in particular? Why do they find cyberspace so damagingly irresistible?

It might be a dangerous combination of peer pressure and inexperience with budgeting. Sophie Brooks, a senior counsellor with the National Debtline, says: 'Young people come under enormous pressure these days to look and be a certain way. They are prepared to

---

The problem often begins at university, when young women build up student loads, overdrafts and credit cards

---

spend small fortunes on getting the right image at a time when they are still learning about managing their money.

'Online marketers know this. So they push their products in a way that sells a whole lifestyle. Inevitably, a lot of young women buy into it, especially when credit is so readily available, it sounds cheap and it seems like everyone else is doing it.' Brooks points out that 'it may be very easy to listen to this and just dismiss it, saying that people should just get a grip and be responsible. But it is not always that easy.'

Some researchers fear a much bigger and more worrying trend. A study by Continental Research claims that Britain has 21m internet addicts and that more than 40 per cent of them are women.

In the next 18 months the number of women logging on is expected to double. Meanwhile, heavily indebted Nicola has some advice based on her bitter experience. 'I would recommend to anybody that they not only don't shop on the web, but that they use credit cards and store cards very warily if at all,' she says.

She acknowledges that some people will spend money regardless, but she says that for someone like her the internet was a temptation too difficult to resist.

But help is at hand for those who think they can cope without getting in too deep. Alan Stevens, head of digital services at Which Online, offers these guidelines to keeping our internet shopping under control:

- Keep one credit card specifically for online purchases and opt for a small limit on it, around £500.
- Don't assume that because something is sold online it is necessarily going to be cheaper. Always compare prices and check the cost of postage and packaging.

- Try to curb spontaneous buying. Weigh up whether you really want or even need the item. Postpone the purchase for 24 hours, or even longer for more expensive items.
- Use the thinking space that comes with internet purchases. You have several days in which you are legally entitled to return the purchase and claim a full refund.
- Use approved shopping sites that adhere to strict standards. So, should something go wrong you have some form of redress.
- The names of the people in debt have been changed. The above article appeared in *The Observer*, 5 August 2001.

© *Guardian Newspapers Limited 2001*

Net shopping hooks army of addicts

Card debt soars as shoppers log on to the store that never closes

By Tracy McVeigh and Amelia Hill

The addictive pull of internet shopping is dragging thousands of victims into a spiral of debt, including thousands of women who have run up huge credit card bills they cannot repay.

The lure of 24-hour access and the explosion in goods and services on offer has seen a 10 per cent increase in credit card debts in the UK this year.

Much of it has been attributed to online spending. The latest report on internet usage shows the number of adults logging on at home has risen from 10 million in October last year to 15.5m this month.

The report by Continental Research, which has monitored internet access in the UK for the past six years, found that while online shopping used to be experimental it is now becoming habitual, especially for women.

Colin Shaddick, who heads the company, said: 'Women are logging on in record numbers – online shopping has certainly played a big role in this.'

The study found that average annual spending online is £700 a year for each internet shopper.

The draw of the internet is especially strong for collectors. Business lecturer Stephen Hall, who has been buying and selling books since he was a child, now has a collection worth £40,000. He is passionate about the opportunities offered by shopping online. 'You can find a book in minutes that you could spend months hunting down at auctions or second-hand bookshops,' he said.

'It can easily become addictive, and all the collectors I know use the internet. I suspect you do waste money because you are less likely to send back a book to Little Rock, Arkansas, than take it back to the high-street shop.'

Like Stephen Hall, most of us can shop online sensibly – but for some it provides an easy, anonymous and accessible way to feed their habit. It also provides secrecy – a central part of any addiction. Dr Samantha Haylett, a psychologist and expert in addiction at the Promis counselling centre, said: 'It's compulsive in the same way as alcohol and gambling, and addicts find themselves completely unable to stop themselves, despite debt mounting and relationships disintegrating. It's the thrill and the buzz of purchasing that overrides all the negative consequences.

'People snigger at shopping addictions, but it's the same as food bingeing: bulimics don't eat nice stuff, or things that are good for them. Shopping addicts are the same: they'll buy things they don't need or want or like. What they're buying is of no importance compared to the thrill they get spending money and acquiring something new.

'I've counselled people who have bought piles of bed linen and curtains and just left them piled up in the corner of the room.

'I have seen people's marriages ruined. There's something more damaging about internet shopping too because it takes place in the home, so the deceit and secrecy is that much closer to the partner who is being deceived.'

Tennis star Serena Williams this year admitted to kicking an internet shopping addiction that saw her spending up to six hours a day online in an attempt to avoid being seen out in public. 'Every day I was in my room and I was online,' Williams said. 'I wasn't able to stop and I bought, bought, bought. I was just out of control.'

Confidence is also growing in online security. Danny Meadows-Klue, chairman of Interactive Advertising Bureau, the internet commercial watchdog, said: 'Online card fraud is a drop in the ocean compared to total credit card fraud, but it is increasing. We want to increase consumer confidence by encouraging shoppers to take simple steps to protect themselves.'

But there are still barriers to online shopping, declares James Goudie, a consumer psychologist at Northumbria University. 'For certain items some people prefer to shop personally, for example to try on an item of clothing and feel the quality. Payment of delivery charges is also off-putting.'

- Promis Centre. 24-hour helpline, 0800 374 318. www.promis.co.uk

- The above article appeared in *The Observer*, 28 October 2001.

© *Guardian Newspapers Limited 2001*

Fake websites boost credit card fraud

By David Bamber, Home Affairs Correspondent

Credit card fraud – particularly on the internet – has soared over the past year, according to a survey to be released next week.

Card fraud will account for £400 million this year, up more than 36 per cent from £293 million in 2000, according to an investigation by the Interactive Advertising Bureau.

In the first seven months of this year, card fraud stood at £250 million, with cases on the internet rising by two-thirds.

Online card fraud this year is expected to account for two per cent of the total, or £8 million, up from £5 million last year – an increase of 60 per cent.

A key area is the growth in fake websites. Criminals have set up websites which look identical to genuine sites but with a slightly different address.

For instance, they will clone a website ending .co.uk and change the address to end with .com or .org. All information put into these fake sites is immediately used to make fraudulent purchases.

Danny Meadows-Klue, the chief executive of the IAB, said: 'Online card fraud may be a drop in the ocean compared to total card fraud but it is rising.

'We want to increase consumer confidence by encouraging shoppers to take simple steps to protect themselves. If online traders take the issue seriously more people will shop online.'

Online shoppers, he said, should double-check the web address of stores they visit. 'Don't be tricked by a number of small but high-profile lookalike or copycat sites,' he said.

Many of the fraudulent sites are based in America or Third World countries, which make them hard to police. Usually they run for only a few days to avoid detection.

For just a couple of hours' work cloning a site, internet thieves can make hundreds of thousands of pounds. Some sites cloned in the recent past include a major bookseller and a sportswear firm. Both of these fake websites have since ceased operation.

> **A key area is the growth in fake websites. Criminals have set up websites which look identical to genuine sites but with a slightly different address**

To detect a copycat site, consumers should look for the small padlock icon at the bottom of a screen.

The icon indicates that a site is secure, registered and that data will be encrypted. In addition, the web address line should include the letters https rather than just http.

The cost of the growth in fraud has been absorbed by credit card companies, which have to guarantee any transaction between £100 to £30,000 under British law.

In reality, these costs are passed on to consumers in higher interest. Openings for fraud can also be cut by vigilance on the part of the consumer.

Mr Meadows-Klue said: 'If a site makes an unusual number of mistakes, has a number of problems or makes unusual claims, don't shop. Forward suspect sites to the IAB.'

He recommends checking a site is legitimate by telephoning the retailer in advance. 'If in doubt, use an alternative method of payment.'

Melanie Hubbard, of Card-watch, the credit card industry fraud prevention organisation, said: 'British banks take the issue of online security very seriously.

'As e-commerce grows, the banks are working alongside retailers and the international card schemes to add further security features and develop new banking services to help this form of trade.'

ADDITIONAL RESOURCES

You might like to contact the following organisations for further information. Due to the increasing cost of postage, many organisations cannot respond to enquiries unless they receive a stamped, addressed envelope.

The Advertising Association
Food Advertising Unit
Abford House
15 Wilton Road
London, SW1V 1NJ
Tel: 020 7828 2771
Fax: 020 7931 0376
E-mail: fau@fau.org.uk
Web site: www.fau.org.uk
The Food Advertising Unit
(FAU), based in the offices of the
UK Advertising Association, is a
centre for information,
communication and research in
the area of food advertising,
particularly TV advertising to
children.

**Advertising Standards Authority
(ASA)**
Brook House
2 Torrington Place
London, WC1E 7HW
Tel: 020 7580 5555
Fax: 020 7631 3051
E-mail: inquiries@asa.org.uk
Web site: www.asa.org.uk
The ASA is the independent, self-
regulatory body for non-broadcast
advertisements in the UK. We
administer the British Codes of
Advertising and Sales Promotion
to ensure that ads are legal, decent,
honest and truthful.

Card Watch
c/o APACS
Mercury House, Triton Court,
14 Finsbury Square
London, EC2A 1LQ
Tel: 020 7711 6356
Fax: 020 7628 0927
E-mail: cardwatch@apacs.org.uk
Web site: www.cardwatch.org.uk
Card Watch is the UK banking
industry's body that works with
police, retailers and organisations
including Crimestoppers to fight
plastic card crime. Card Watch is
run under the Association for
Payment Clearing Services
(APACS), the banking industry
body overseeing money
transmission and payment clearing

activities in the UK. Its members
are the major high street banks and
building societies.

**Consumer Credit Counselling
Service (CCCS)**
Wade House
Merrion Centre
Leeds, LS2 8NG
Tel: 0113 297 0121
E-mail: info@cccs.co.uk
Web site: www.cccs.co.uk
Consumer Credit Counselling
Service (CCCS) is a registered
charity whose purpose is to assist
families and individuals who are in
financial difficulty by providing
independent and confidential
counselling on personal budgeting,
advice on the wise use of credit
and, where appropriate, achievable
plans to repay outstanding debts.
For free, confidential debt advice
call 0800 138 1111.

**National Association of Citizens'
Advice Bureaux**
Myddleton House
115-123 Pentonville
London, N1 9LZ
Tel: 020 7833 2181
Fax: 020 7833 4367
Web site: www.nacab.org.uk
www.adviceguide.org.uk
The Citizens' Advice Bureau
Service offers free, confidential,
impartial and independent advice.
From its origins in 1939 as an
emergency service during World
War II, it has evolved into a
professional national agency.

National Youth Agency (NYA)
17-23 Albion Street
Leicester, LE1 6GD
Tel: 0116 285 3700
Fax: 0116 285 3777
E-mail: nya@nya.org.uk
Web site: www.nya.org.uk
The National Youth Agency aims
to advance youth work to promote
young people's personal and social
development, and their voice,
influence and place in society.
Produces the publication *Young
People Now*.

Office of Fair Trading (OFT)
Fleetbank House
2-6 Salisbury Square
London, EC4Y 8JX
Tel: 020 7211 8000
Helpline 0345 224499
Fax: 020 7211 8800
E-mail: enquiries@oft.gov.uk
Web site: www.oft.gov.uk
Student web site: www.ofthelp.com
The OFT is responsible for making
markets work well for consumers.
They achieve this by promoting
and protecting consumer interests
throughout the UK, while ensuring
that businesses are fair and
competitive.

Trading Standards Institute (TSI)
4/5 Hadleigh Business Centre
351 London Road
Hadleigh
Essex, SS7 2BT
Tel: 0870 872 9000
Fax: 0870 872 9025
E-mail: institute@tsi.org.uk
Web site:
www.tradingstandards.gov.uk
The Trading Standards Institute
(formerly the Institute of Trading
Standards Administration ITSA)
has represented the interests of
Trading Standards professionals for
120 years. We have a long and
proud history of ensuring that the
views of our members are well
represented at the highest level of
government, both nationally and
internationally.

INDEX

ACKNOWLEDGEMENTS

The publisher is grateful for permission to reproduce the following material.

While every care has been taken to trace and acknowledge copyright, the publisher tenders its apology for any accidental infringement or where copyright has proved untraceable. The publisher would be pleased to come to a suitable arrangement in any such case with the rightful owner.

Chapter One: Consumer Trends

Consumers splash out in 'feelgood revolution', © Guardian Newspapers Limited 2001, *No time like the present for debts, drink and decorating*, © Guardian Newspapers Limited 2001, *Insights into consumer markets*, © MORI, *Average weekly expenditure on the main commodities and services*, © Crown Copyright is reproduced with the permission of the Controller of Her Majesty's Stationery Office, *Shopping daze*, © The Daily Mail, 2001, *Commercial pressure*, © The Food Advertising Unit, The Advertising Association, *Why UK consumers are on a spending spree*, © Guardian Newspapers Limited 2001, *Children and advertising*, © Advertising Standards Authority, *Forget flying the flag. We're all global now*, © Guardian Newspapers Limited 2001, *Interbrand/ Business Week ranking of 40 of the World's Most Valuable Brands*, © Interbrand, *The way we live now*, © Guardian Newspapers Limited 2001, *Richest 10% spend seven times more than poorest*, © Guardian Newspapers Limited 2001.

Chapter Two: Consumer Awareness

Your rights as a consumer, © Telegraph Group Limited, London 2001, *Basic consumer rights*, © MORI, *Survey results*, © MORI, *General consumer rights*, © Crown Copyright is reproduced with the permission of the Controller of Her Majesty's Stationery Office, *I don't believe it!*, © Guardian Newspapers Limited 2001, *Shops in the wrong over your rights*, © Guardian Newspapers Limited 2001, *Consumer wrongs*, © Trading Standards Institute (TSI), *How to complain*, © Crown Copyright is reproduced with the permission of the Controller of Her Majesty's Stationery Office, *Would you credit it?*, © National Youth Agency, *Limits to your rights*, © Crown Copyright is reproduced with the permission of the Controller of Her Majesty's Stationery Office, *Types of fraud*, © Card Watch, *Top tips*, © Card Watch, *Dealing with credit*, © Crown Copyright is reproduced with the permission of the Controller of Her Majesty's Stationery Office, *Ways to pay*, © Trading Standards Institute (TSI), *Who owes all the money?*, © Consumer Credit Counselling Service (CCCS), *Total debt*, © Consumer Credit Counselling Service (CCCS), *Credit and debts*, © Crown Copyright is reproduced with the permission of the Controller of Her Majesty's Stationery Office, *Seeking help with debt*, © National Association of Citizens' Advice Bureaux, *Preventing fraud*, © Card Watch, *Internet shopping*, © Card Watch, *Young, single – and £15,000 in the red*, © Guardian Newspapers Limited 2001, *Net shopping hooks army of addicts*, © Guardian Newspapers Limited 2001, *Fake websites boost credit card fraud*, © Telegraph Group Limited, London 2001.

Photographs and illustrations:

Pages 1, 6, 14, 32 35: Bev Aisbett, pages 2, 13, 22, 29, 37 40: Simon Kneebone, pages 5, 20, 27: Pumpkin House, pages 17, 19, 25: Fiona Katauskas.

Craig Donnellan
Cambridge
April, 2002